Wallace Library

DUE DATE (stamped in blue)
RETURN DATE (stamped in black)

AMERICAN EDUCATION

Its Men

Ideas

and

Institutions

Advisory Editor

Lawrence A. Cremin
Frederick A. P. Barnard Professor of Education
Teachers College, Columbia University

Parish Education
in
Colonial Virginia

Guy Fred Wells

ARNO PRESS & THE NEW YORK TIMES
New York * *1969*

Reprint edition 1969 by Arno Press, Inc.

*

Library of Congress Catalog Card No. 71-89252

*

Reprinted from a copy in Teachers College Library

*

Manufactured in the United States of America

Editorial Note

AMERICAN EDUCATION: *Its Men, Institutions and Ideas* presents selected works of thought and scholarship that have long been out of print or otherwise unavailable. Inevitably, such works will include particular ideas and doctrines that have been outmoded or superseded by more recent research. Nevertheless, all retain their place in the literature, having influenced educational thought and practice in their own time and having provided the basis for subsequent scholarship.

Lawrence A. Cremin
Teachers College

Parish Education
in
Colonial Virginia

PARISH EDUCATION IN COLONIAL VIRGINIA

By

GUY FRED WELLS, Ph.D.

Submitted in
Partial Fulfillment of the Requirements
for the Degree of Doctor of Philosophy,
in the Faculty of Philosophy,
Columbia University

Published by
𝕿eachers 𝕮ollege, 𝕮olumbia 𝖀niversity
New York City
1923

ACKNOWLEDGMENTS

The author of this study is indebted to Professor Paul Monroe for suggesting its subject and for assisting in the work of locating sources and organizing material. He is under obligation to several of the ministers of the Episcopal Church in Virginia who aided in the search for parish vestry books and gave access to those in their possession. Acknowledgment should also be made of the courtesy of the librarian at the Episcopal Theological Seminary at Alexandria, Virginia, in making available for examination the collection of parish records in her keeping.

CONTENTS

INTRODUCTION

Public participation in education in England at the time of the settlement of the American colonies consisted chiefly in the provisions for instructing the poor which were made by the parishes as the governmental organizations responsible for the care of dependents. There was little uniformity of practice among the parishes, but it was not unusual for one to supply a teacher, provide a school room, pay for the tuition of poor children in a private school, or conduct a workhouse in which instruction was given. In rare instances a school was established and supported out of the rates. Probably no single parish used all these means of aiding in the education of its poor children, and many may have made no provision whatever, but the use of parish funds for educational purposes was sufficiently common to furnish the colonists in America with a definite precedent in public support.[1]

With the English custom as a basis, the New England towns, which had their origin in the parishes of the mother country, established schools for all classes of children. Their action was due to a combination of favoring circumstances, which besides the precedents included the compact settlement in towns, an approximate equality of status among the inhabitants, a uniformity of religious belief which embraced the doctrine that all should be able to read the Bible, and a relatively high average of intelligence.

The factors in the situation in New England which brought about the establishment of public schools for all children did not exist together in any other section of the country. In Virginia the social and economic distinctions and the wide distribution of the population made impossible the development of common schools, but a consideration of the general conformity of ideas and institutions in the colony to those in England makes it seem reasonable to presume that in education the familiar custom of providing more or less adequately

---

[1]For a discussion of English precedents see Fish, C. R., "The English Parish and Education at the Beginning of American Colonization," *School Review*, Vol. XXIII, p. 433.

that doe not take the oath of allegiance and supremacy to his majesty and sub-
scribe to the doctrine and discipline of the Church of England.

Act III.   That the churchwardens shall twice every yeare (*viz.*) in December
court and April court deliver a true presentment in writing of such misdemeanors
as to their knowledge, or by common fame have beene committed whilst they have
been churchwardens.

Here is given a list of moral and religious misdemeanors including
swearing, sabbath abusing, drunkenness, slander, and adultery.

Act XIV.   And be it further enacted That the said churchwardens take care and
be impowered during their churchwardenship to keepe the church in repaire
provide books and ornaments. . . and that they the said churchwardens doe
faithfully collect the ministers dues, cause them to be brought to convenient
places and honestly pay them, and that of all the disbursements and receipts they
give a true account to the vestry when by them required.[2]

THE RELATION OF VESTRY AND WARDENS

The above regulations do not indicate clearly the intended relation between the wardens and the vestry, for while the vestry was
made responsible for the election of the wardens and for "the more
orderly manageing of all parociall affaires," the wardens were given
apparently independent obligations without any suggestion of their
subordination to the vestry except that they should submit their
accounts when called upon to do so.   The probability is that the
legislators had in mind no definite theory of division of power, and
that in giving the wardens a status of apparent independence they
were moved merely by a knowledge of English custom and a consideration of the necessity of having certain officers representative of the
parish and vestry who could be held directly responsible for the
execution of important functions more readily than the vestry as a
whole.[3]

Whatever was the intention back of the laws, the important fact
is that in practice the vestries did not hesitate to assume the initiative
in the exercise of any of the functions of parish government and order
the wardens to take the action they determined upon, regardless of
the evident meaning of the law.   As a typical instance showing the
control often exercised by the vestry over the wardens even in the

---

[2]Hening, *Statutes at Large*, II, pp. 43–45.
[3]In England the vestry was compelled to vote the taxes to defray expenses incurred by the wardens in the care of the church and the poor (Webb, *English
Local Government*, p. 39).

conduct of minor church business which in law was given to the wardens, there is an order of the vestry of St. Mark's Parish requiring the wardens to buy two prayer books.[4] The fact that the wardens were chosen by their associates in the vestry, a close corporation, and that the vestry was responsible for voting taxes, no doubt tended to make them merely representative or executive officials. This does not mean that they seldom exercised initiative or that they could not be punished by the county court for failure to carry out their obligations as indicated in the law. It merely means that in practice they were subject to vestry control, that what they did was with the understood allowance of the vestry, and that they might be given detailed directions or allowed considerable freedom.

THE VESTRY

The provision in the law of 1661–62 that the membership of the vestry should be made up "of the most able men of each parish," while of little real force in itself, was generally adhered to under the favoring circumstances of the situation, as is suggested by the fact that practically all the prominent Virginians were at one time or another and often for long periods members of the vestry in their respective parishes.[5] A typical case is that of George Washington, who was elected to membership in the Truro Parish vestry in 1762.[6] In the choice of twelve as the appropriate number of men to constitute a vestry there is very probably a reflection of the practice followed in certain parts of rural England in the seventeenth century, although consideration was no doubt given to the fact that this number secured adequate representation of the parish without making the vestry so large as to be unwieldy.[7]

---

[4]Slaughter, *St. Mark's Parish*, p. 33.

[5]Truro Parish in Westmoreland County in its early history furnishes an exception to the general rule both as to qualifications and number of men in the vestry. In 1744 there were sixteen men present at the vestry meeting, and in that year Lawrence Washington sent a protest to the Assembly against the vestry, complaining that they were not able to read and write and were not otherwise qualified. As a result the vestry was dissolved and a new body elected (Hening, V, pp. 274–75; Slaughter, *History of Truro Parish*, p. 20). The record of Kingston Parish in Gloucester County, which begins in 1679, shows the attendance at the vestry meeting of the vestrymen and "Inhabitants."

[6]"1762, October 25th. Ordered, that George Washington Esqr. be chosen one of the Vestrymen of this Parish in the room of William Pecke Gent. deceased" (Slaughter, *History of Truro Parish*, p. 122).

[7]Webb, in his *English Local Government*, p. 179, says: In the counties of Northumberland and Durham we find the parish government, for the past three centuries, normally in the hands of a body known as "The Four-and-Twenty" (or

The vestry was made a self-perpetuating body by the regulation in Act II, quoted above, which deals with the filling of vacancies, and there was no deviation from this arrangement except when some special circumstance like the changing of the bounds of a parish or the illegal acts of the vestry made it necessary for the Assembly to dissolve the vestry and to hold a new election.[8] Bacon's Assembly in 1676 endeavored to change the custom by providing for the election of vestrymen every three years, but the law enacted was repealed in the following year upon Berkeley's return to power, and the statute of 1661–62 remained in force.[9] There is no evidence to show that after Bacon's time there was any protest against the system of parish government which kept the control in the hands of an oligarchy, but it must have seemed oppressive to many in the middle and lower classes not represented in the vestry.[10] While in England only a

---

occasionally, "The Twelve"). . . .The number twelve seems to have been less usual than twenty-four. It occurs in Durham, at Pittington, and Stainton; and in Northumberland, at Haltwhistle; and at Bywell St. Andrew.

[8]In 1757 the vestry of Dettingen Parish was dissolved and an election ordered because the vestry had "been guilty of many illegal practices very oppressive to the inhabitants" (Hening, VII, 145).

What was the general practice in conducting the parish elections cannot be determined from the parish records. When Truro Parish was divided in 1765 what was in effect a primary was first held, and then later there was an election in which those who had received the largest number of votes in the primary were voted upon, each man being allowed to vote for twelve. The original record of this election, now in the Congressional Library, was kept by George Washington (Slaughter, *History of Truro Parish*, p. 44).

[9]Hening, II, 380.

[10]That the vestries were close corporations is the view generally held by writers on Virginia colonial history, but Bruce, who is the leading authority on Virginia in the 17th century, holds that in the early part of the colonial period the vestries were elected at intervals by the inhabitants, and that this was the practice after Bacon's Rebellion down to the end of the 17th century at least. In his *Institutional History of Virginia in the 17th Century*, Vol. I, p. 67, he says that before Bacon's time the vestries had assumed the power of cooption, but that after the pacification of the Colony in 1677, "the power of self-perpetuation without popular elections at intervals, to which apparently they had no real claim either in law or custom, seems to have passed from the vestries." He further states that "at the end of the century, the vestries were chosen by the suffrage of the freeholders and householders; but in the intervals between the elections of the entire body by a popular vote" the vestrymen could fill the vacancies caused by death or removal from the parish (p. 70), implying that it was the custom at the end of the century to have occasional elections.

Beverley, writing on the situation at the end of the 17th century, says, "These Vestries consist of twelve Gentlemen of the Parish, and were at first chosen by the vote of the Parishioners; but upon the Death of any, have been continued by the Survivors electing another in his place" (*History of Virginia*, p. 227). In *The Present State of Virginia*, written by Hartwell, Chilton, and Blair in 1697, it is stated that the vestries "have a power to continue themselves, for as one dyes or removes out of the Parish, the remaining Vestrymen chuse another in his room" (p. 65).

With reference to the law, to which Bruce refers as being opposed to the idea of

relatively few paid parish taxes,[11] in Virginia all freemen above the age of sixteen were levied upon.

In the management of church affairs the vestry took care of the matters delegated to it in the laws of 1661-62, which have been quoted, and in addition it chose the minister and readers, bought and equipped the minister's glebe, and to a greater or less extent directed the wardens in the exercise of the ecclesiastical functions delegated in law to them. The chief civil responsibilities of the vestry were the laying of the parish levy and the care of the poor. Each fall it voted a tax to cover parish expenses, the larger share of which ordinarily went to the payment of the minister and to poor support.[12] Although in England the wardens with the overseers of the poor were the responsible poor law officials with power to levy a rate for the poor without vestry control, in Virginia they acted as representatives of the vestry. Late in the colonial period a number of vestries established workhouses for the care and employment of the poor.[13]

There were laws enacted after 1662 specifically empowering the wardens to bind out illegitimate children upon their own responsibility and also poor, neglected children upon certificate from the county court, but the vestry books show that wherever the vestries

---

a close vestry, it may be said that the law of 1661–62 above quoted gave legal justification for cooption. It was this law which Bacon changed, and if it had not been the custom before he obtained control there would have been no occasion for changing the law. That the close vestry was very common in England is demonstrated by Webb (*English Local Government*, pp. 175–76). After showing that there were many variations in the organization of parish government in England, he says with reference to the close vestry in certain counties, "It may almost be described as the typical form of parish government in town and country alike" (p. 175).

As evidence that vestries in Virginia were not self-perpetuating after 1677, Bruce refers to two cases, that of North Farnham Parish and a parish in Northampton County. He says, "In 1692 the justices of Rappahannock appointed a day for the inhabitants of North Farnham Parish" to assemble for a popular election (p. 68). In 1092 Rappahannock County was discontinued and Richmond and Essex made out of it. This reorganization probably meant some change in the boundaries of the parishes involved, and in any case it was the occasion for the election. The special occasion for the election of a vestry in the parish in Northampton County in 1691 was that two parishes which had existed separately after 1642 were reunited in 1691 (Meade, *Old Churches*, I, p. 258). It can readily be seen that neither of the two cases mentioned serves as a basis for the view that after 1677 the vestries were commonly chosen by popular election.

[11]Webb, *English Local Government*, p. 48.

[12]The vestry books show that ordinarily the vestrymen were much interested in the welfare of the indigent poor, but occasionally toward the end of the colonial period records like the following appear: "Order'd That the Churchwardens do let out the poor of this parish to the lowest bidder" (*Bristol Parish Vestry Book*, p. 182).

[13]See Chapter IV.

wished they considered the cases and ordered the wardens to act in accordance 'with their decision.   This was justified by the general principle that the wardens were subject to vestry control, and by the fact that the vestry was responsible for the care of the poor and for parish finances.   The vestry also often ordered the apprenticing of orphans, although the laws provided that this duty should be performed by the county court.   There was no statute giving the vestry the right to provide out of parish funds for the schooling of poor children, but this was occasionally done, and as in England, it is probable that there would have been no legal interference if a vestry had consistently made expenditure for the purpose.

One of the important duties of the vestry was to appoint men every four years to go over the bounds of estates and renew the marks.[14]   In some of the vestry books the record of processionings takes up more space than any other item.   A law of 1723 required the vestries to divide the parishes into precincts and appoint men in each to examine the growing tobacco and make certain that the quality was being maintained.   The highways were in charge of county surveyors who were appointed by the justices, but the vestries were enjoined to order the parishioners to supply men to aid the surveyors.

The vestry books contain numerous illustrations of the fact that in the exercise of civil functions the vestries went beyond the powers specifically delegated to them in law.   The vestry of St. Paul's Parish in Hanover County in 1707 built an almshouse;[15]   Bristol Parish Vestry in 1732 "Order'd that a Causeway be Built from the Ferry Landing to the Chanell on the South Side," and in 1766 it fined a man "for selling Corn by unlawful measure;"[16] the vestry of Upper Parish in Nansemond County in 1769 paid "to Samuel Wallis for schooling some poor children" six pounds.[17]

The work of presenting cases of moral or religious delinquency was generally left in the hands of the wardens, although there is sufficient evidence to show that when it seemed advisable to the vestry it first examined the facts of a case and then ordered the wardens to act as it determined.[18]   In St Peter's Parish in 1734 the vestry took upon itself not only the accusation but also the punishment of offenders

[14]Hening, II, 101.
[15]MS. vestry minutes of St. Paul's Parish for 1707.
[16]Bristol Parish vestry book, pp. 61, 217.
[17]Upper Parish MS. vestry book, record for 1769.
[18]Bruce, *Institutional History of Virginia*, I, 82.

against church decorum and ordered the wardens to "cause a good and substantial Pair of Stocks to be forthwith erected near the Church-Yard Wall."[19] In the eighteenth century there was generally less concern over the misdemeanors listed in the law of 1661–62 than there had been before,[20] and the grand jury took from the parish officials the responsibility for the more serious offenses.[21]

THE CHURCH WARDENS

It has been shown that in general the wardens acted as representatives of the vestry, and that the position of independence which Acts XIII and XIV in the code of 1661–62 seemed to give them was in practice not held, for it was always qualified by the right of the vestry to direct them.   In the ordinary course of events the wardens, after their election in the fall meeting, collected the parish levy of tobacco,[22] paid the parish servants and the people who had taken care of the poor during the year just ended, and made other expenditures which had been sanctioned by the vestry.   They carried out the orders of the vestry with regard to placing of the poor for the year, ordered brought before them for indenturing the children whose apprenticeship had been ordered by the vestry or court, and presented to the county court the names of persons who were judged by themselves or the vestry to be presumably guilty of moral or religious offense.   Whatever other orders were made by the vestry with regard to the repair or the equipment of the churches, chapels, or glebe buildings, or any other matter were carried out.

During the course of the year the wardens extended aid to the poor in cases of emergency for which provision had not been made. At the spring vestry meeting in some parishes they made up their accounts with the vestry.   In preparation for the fall meeting at the end of the year of service they prepared a list of parish expenses to be submitted to the vestry, and either at this meeting or the one held in the spring they probably turned over to the vestry clerk the apprenticeship indentures and other contracts to which they had been

---

[19]St. Peter's Parish MS. vestry minutes, p. 170.

[20]See *The Present State of Virginia*, by Hartwell, Chilton, and Blair, p. 66; *Autobiography of Devereux Jarratt*, p. 21; "Journal of Philip Fithian," *Amer. Hist. Rev.*, V, p. 294.

[21]Ingle, E., *Local Institutions of Virginia*, Johns Hopkins University Studies, 1885, p. 70.

[22]In some parishes, particularly toward the end of the colonial period, the vestries appointed the county sheriff as parish tax collector.   In St. Paul's Parish in 1706 it was "Ordered that Capt. Roger Thompson, high sheriff for the present year of New Kent County, collect the parish Tob." (MS. vestry minutes, p. 14).

a party.   If the vestry or wardens were accused by the court of some delinquency in carrying out the laws the wardens might be called before the court to answer the charge.

SERVANTS OF THE PARISH

Each parish had as paid minor officers a vestry clerk, one or more readers, and one or more sextons.[23]   The vestry clerk kept the vestry records, and the sextons performed the duties usually associated with their office.   The parish church and each of the chapels, which were built for the convenience of the parishioners living in the outlying districts, had a lay reader to read the service in the absence of the minister, who conducted service alternately in the different places of worship.[24]   In indicating the custom in 1705, Beverley said,

If a parish be of greater Extent than ordinary, it hath generally a Chapel of Ease; and some of the Parishes have two Such Chapels, besides the church for the greater convenience of the Parishioners.   In these Chapels the Minister preaches alternately, always leaving a Reader, to Read Prayers when he can't attend himself.[25]

Although the reader's primary function was to act as a minister's substitute in his absence or in case of vacancy in the ministerial office, he sometimes, and perhaps usually, assisted in the performance of the service when the minister was present.   He also more or less often kept the parish register of births, marriages, and deaths, took immediate responsibility for the care of his chapel, and catechized children and servants.   As assistant his work was like that of the parish clerk in England in the seventeenth and eighteenth centuries, and in fact he was often referred to as "the clerk."[26]   A typical illustration of the use of the term "clerk" in reference to the reader is found

[23]Occasionally the offices of vestry clerk, reader, and sexton were held by one person.   For instance in Bristol Parish in 1762 the vestry ordered the payment of 2400 pounds of tobacco as a year's salary "To William Yarbrough Clk of the Brick Church, Vestry and Sexton" (Bristol Parish Vestry Book, p. 183).

[24]In the early days parishes had only one reader, but in the eighteenth century, as the number of chapels was increased, the larger and more populous among them sometimes had as many as four.

[25]Beverley, Robert, *History of Virginia*, p. 226.

[26]The parish clerk in England held an office "halfway between that of a curate and a church menial."   In the 15th and 16th centuries he was commonly a cleric whose main duty it was to serve as general assistant to the minister or priest. He took a minor part in the church service, arrayed the shoulders of the minister with the surplice, sometimes acted as bell-ringer, and performed other menial duties.   In the 17th century the position of parish clerk came to be filled more and more often by an uneducated layman, and finally in 1739 the court definitely held that he was a temporal officer (Webb, *English Local Government*, pp. 32–33).

in the following quotation from Hugh Jones' *Present State of Virginia*.

The clerk in case of the minister's death or absence has great business, and is a kind of curate, performing frequently all of the offices of the church, except the two sacraments and matrimony; . . . In some places they read the lessons, publish the banns, ec. when the minister is present, for his ease; which first may not be improper in very hot weather, or if the minister be sick or infirm, if the clerk can read tolerably well. . . .[27]

Because of the fact that the reader was often referred to as "the clerk," it has been understood by some that he was usually a trained cleric or a young man studying for orders, and with this understanding as a basis it has been assumed that during the week in his spare time he acted as a public parish teacher. The possibility of his having served as a teacher makes it necessary, in an inquiry into parish educational activity, to examine somewhat carefully into his status. In fact there is nothing to show that the reader or clerk was more than an ordinary layman with some regular secular occupation, whose work in conducting Sunday service or assisting the minister was a minor interest. Bishop Meade, who made a most careful study of the Church in the colonial period, makes no mention of the clerk as a trained cleric except in three or four cases where the circumstances were unusual and the arrangements temporary.[28] One of the very few cases which have been found is that of Nathaniel Eaton, the first head of Harvard College, who came to Accomac after his dismissal from Harvard in 1639 and served there for a time as parish clerk.[29]

---

[27]*Present State of Virginia* (1725), p. 67. Another typical illustration of the use of the term is found in the diary of Philip Fithian ("Journal of Philip Fithian," *Amer. Hist. Rev.*, V, p. 294). Fithian said that it was customary for the gentlemen to go into church in a body after the service had begun, and that he had "known the clerk to come out and call them in to prayers."
   The only reference to the clerk or reader as a "parish clerk" found in the course of the present study occurs in a memorandum of Governor Nicholson: "A small encouragem't to the Parish Clerk or reader may perhaps enable him to keep such a school" (*Va. Mag. of Hist. and Biog.*, VII, p. 157).
[28]Meade, *Old Churches and Families of Virginia*.
[29]Wise, J. C., *Early History of the Eastern Shore*, p. 261.
   The idea that there were in colonial Virginia many young clerics who might be supposed to have acted as minister's assistant is suggested in "A List of Emigrant Ministers to America," compiled by Gerald Fothergill from the books of the Lords of the Treasury. The list contains the names of some 1200 men who went to America between 1690 and 1811, each of whom received from the Treasury 20£ as passage money. In many cases the word "clerk" appears after the name of a recipient, and it might be understood that where this occurs we have the name of a man who was not an ordained minister, but one who, possibly as a deacon, came over to act as a parish clerk or assistant to a minister. "Clerk" as used in this connection, however, indicated only that the person to whom it was applied belonged to the clerical profession. Following are illustrations of its use in this

The moral qualifications of the reader are indicated in a law appearing in the code of 1661–62:

That every parish not haveing a minister to officiate every Sunday make choice of a grave and sober person of good life and conversation to read divine service every intervening Sunday at the Parish church, when the minister preacheth at any other place.[30]

The ability to read acceptably was implied, and it is very probable that in making a choice from among candidates who were orthodox and morally qualified this was the distinguishing trait considered, as is suggested by the following record from the Bristol Parish vestry book:

Ordered that Nathaniell Parrott be Discontinued as Clerk of Sapponie Chapple and That there be a publick Notice given for persons to appear at ye ferry Chapple To Try for ye Same on Monday ye 19th of this Instant   (Nov. 12, 1733).

The vestrymen were evidently "To Try" candidates to determine their reading ability.   There is no direct evidence showing what was the custom in Virginia, but, as will be shown in Chapter II, it is very probable that school-masters were often chosen as readers because

---

general sense.   The church wardens of Elizabeth River Parish in Lower Norfolk County in 1645, "exhibited there presentment against Mr. Thomas Harrison, Clark (Parson of the Said parish) for not reading the book of common Prayer." (Lower Norfolk County Court Records, quoted in *Lower Norfolk County Antiquary*, II, p. 12).   In a patent issued to Farnefold Nutt appears the following record: "John Farnefold, clerk, by his last will gave one hundred acres f or ye use f a Free School" (Northern Neck Land Book, quoted in *Virginia Historical Magazine*, I, p. 216).   Farnefold was minister in St. Stephen's Parish from 1680 until his death in 1702 (*William and Mary College Quarterly*, XVII, p. 245). In an act passed in South Carolina in 1710–11 provision is made for the support of an aged minister—"Whereas Atkin Williamson, Clerk, is grown so disabled with age, sickness, and other infirmities, that he cannot any longer attend the duty of his ministerial functions. . . ." (Dalcho, *History of the Episcopal Church in S. C.*, p. 454).

Fothergill states that each man in his list was sent "to some definite cure," but it is impossible to determine from the existing lists of ministers serving in Virginia just when each man took up his work.   It can be shown, however, that a number of the 39 "clerks" mentioned by Fothergill as going to the colony were parish pastors within a year or two after passage money had been provided for them.   The following are typical cases:

"Richard Squire, clerk," sailing after Nov. 30, 1702, was minister in St. Peter's Parish, New Kent County, in 1703 (Meade, I, 385).

"Yates [probably Robert Yates], clerk," sailing after Jan. 3, 1689–99, was minister in Christ Church Parish, Middlesex County, in 1699 (Meade, I, 359).

"Patrick Falconer, clerk," sailing after April 29, 1710, was minister in Hungar's Parish in Northampton County in 1712 (Meade, I, 258).

"James Robertson, clerk," sailing after Jan. 15, 1717–18, was a minister in Virginia in 1719 (Meade, II, 393).

It is certain in view of the above facts that the term "clerk" was used by the Treasury recorder in its general sense to indicate a cleric.

[30]Hening, II, 46–47.

they possessed the requisite qualifications and because they were interested in the stipend attached to the position.

THE NUMBER AND SIZE OF THE PARISHES

In general the institution of new parishes followed the growth and spread of population. In 1649 it was reported that there were twenty churches in the colony, and there were probably as many parishes.[31] In 1697 there were fifty parishes,[32] and at the end of the colonial period approximately ninety had been organized.[33]

The parishes varied much in size; some embraced two large counties, while others took up only one-third or one-half of a small county. As the density of population increased the larger parishes were reduced in size. The best description of the situation with respect to the size and population of the parishes at any time appears in a report to the Bishop of London made by the ministers in 1724.[34] Although only twenty-nine were reported upon, those for which the facts were given were in general the older, smaller parishes. The average area was approximately four hundred and ten square miles, with an average population of somewhat over two hundred families. Variations in size were between fourteen hundred and one hundred square miles, and in number of families between four hundred and thirty and seventy-eight.

THE PARISH RECORDS

The official records of the parish government were kept in the "vestry book," which contained the minutes of the vestry meetings, the record of the processionings of the bounds of lands, and sometimes the copies of the apprenticeship contracts to which the wardens were a party. There was also a "register" in which the minister or reader recorded births, marriages, and deaths, but this held nothing in regard to governmental activity.

The minutes of the vestry meetings, kept by the vestry clerk, show the conclusions reached by the vestry with reference to the various matters which came before it, without there being any indication of the votes or the considerations which moved the vestry to act. It is usually impossible to tell which items of business were brought up by the wardens and which by other members of the vestry, there

---

[31]*A Perfect Description of Virginia* (1649), Force Historical Tracts, II, p. 8.
[32]Hartwell, Chilton, and Blair, *The Present State of Virginia*, p. 64.
[33]Meade, *Old Churches*, I, p. 17.
[34]Perry, *Historical Collections*, I, pp. 261–312.

seldom being a record of the wardens' reports to the vestry.   Most of the minutes are in the form of orders to make expenditures in payment of parish obligations and to provide for the poor in appropriate ways.   Aside from the list of expenditures, the minutes record the number of tithables each year, the tax rate, the names of the members present, the appointment of officers, the arrangements made for constructing or repairing parish buildings, and directions given the wardens concerning the apprenticing of poor children.   Occasionally there is a report of a committee, a petition to the Assembly, or the record of a fine received.

In England the wardens' account books constitute a most important source of information concerning parish government in the seventeenth and eighteenth centuries,[35] but in Virginia the subjection of the wardens to vestry control and the fact that most of their work was in execution of the vestry's orders made it unnecessary to have a permanent record of their activities except that contained in the vestry book.   The apprenticeship indentures in the cases of children bound out by order of the vestry were ordinarily given to the vestry clerk for preservation or record.   This was sometimes, and probably commonly, the case where the indentures were made out "upon certificate" from the county court.

After the dissolution of parish government and the separation of church and state at the end of the colonial period, the vestry books were no longer used for recording civil business except in several cases where the overseers of the poor continued the accounts recording payments for the support of the poor, but the vestries of some of the Episcopal churches which were organized on the new basis kept up in the old books the record of church transactions.   The chief practical value of the colonial vestry books in the succeeding years was in the aid which the record of processionings gave in the establishment of land claims.   Bishop Meade, who, when in pursuit of his study of Episcopal Church history in Virginia, made a systematic attempt to locate the vestry books, said in 1857, "The vestry books from which I could have gotten much, and some of which I have seen, are, for the most part, either lost, or fallen into the hands of persons who use them for the establishment of land claims or bounties."   The books of which he obtained possession were deposited at his death in the

---

[35]Webb, *English Local Government*, pp. 7, 114.

library of the Episcopal Seminary at Alexandria.[36] In 1880 Bishop Slaughter, then historiographer of the diocese of Virginia, made a report to the council of the Episcopal church showing the results of his systematic endeavor to locate the vestry books then in existence. He reported the location of nineteen of them, most of which were at Alexandria.[37] Since 1880 other vestry books have been found, making a total of thirty-six. Only those of Henrico Parish and Bristol Parish have been printed. Except in the course of the present study no recent systematic attempt has been made to locate the records or to study them as a whole.

Below is a list of the vestry books the existence and location of which are known. It represents nearly half of the parishes in existence in the latter part of the colonial period and all sections of the colony. Only four contain a record of parish activities before 1700.

Albemarle in Sussex County, 1741–1784; Episcopal Seminary, Alexandria.

Antrim in Halifax, 1752–1817; Alexandria.

Augusta in Augusta, 1747–1780; County Clerk's office, Staunton.

Blissland in New Kent, 1721–1787; Alexandria.

Bristol in Prince George, 1720–1789; library of Rev. Churchill Gibson; reprint edited by C. G. Chamberlayne.

Bruton in James City; original destroyed; *Church Review and Ecclesiastical Register*, VIII, 1855–1856, gives extracts from records from 1674 on.

Camden in Pittsylvania, 1767–1777; Mrs. M. E. Clement, Chatham, Virginia.

Christ Church in Lancaster, 1739–1786; Alexandria.

Christ Church in Middlesex, 1663–1787; Alexandria.

Cumberland in Lunenburg, 1747–1784; Alexandria.

Dettingen in Prince William, 1748–1802; Alexandria.

Elizabeth City in Elizabeth City, 1751–1780; Rev. C. B. Bryan, Petersburg.

Elizabeth River in Norfolk, 1749–1761; County Clerk's office, Norfolk.

Frederick in Frederick, 1764–1816; Alexandria.

Fredericksville in Louisa, 1742–1787; Alexandria.

Henrico in Henrico, 1730–1773; in possession of vestry of St. John's Church, Richmond; reprint in Wynne's *Historical Documents from the Old Dominion*.

Hungar's in Northampton, 1634–1700; County Clerk's office, Eastville, Virginia; 1754–1780, Episcopal Church rectory, Eastville.

King William in Powhatan (later Henrico), 1707–1750; Miss Lelia Walker, Ft. Estell, Kentucky; translation from French, in which the record was kept, in *Virginia Magazine of History and Biography*, XI, XII, XIII.

Kingston in Mathews, 1679–1796; Alexandria.

Lexington in Amherst, 1779–1880; Alexandria.

Linhaven in Norfolk, 1723–1779; copy in hands of Rev. C. B. Bryan, Petersburg.

[36]*Virginia Magazine of History*, III, p. 85.
[37]*Journal of the 85th Annual Council of the Episcopal Church in Virginia*, pp. 81–86.

Lower Parish, Nansemond County, 1749–1784; County Clerk's office.
Newport in Isle of Wight, 1724–1776; Isle of Wight County Court House, Isle of Wight, Virginia.
Petsworth in Gloucester, 1677–1793; copy in possession of Virginia Historical Society, Richmond.
St. Andrew's in Brunswick, 1746–1782; office of County Clerk, Lawrenceville.
St. George's in Spottsylvania, 1726–1800; Episcopal rectory, Fredericksburg.
St. James in Goochland, 1744–1860; Alexandria.
St. Mark's in Culpeper, 1730–1778 (record for 1753–7 torn out); Alexandria.
St. Paul's in Hanover and New Kent, 1755–1774; Alexandria.
St. Peter's in New Kent, 1686–1759; Alexandria.
Shelburne in Loudon, 1771–1805; Alexandria.
South Farnham in Essex, 1739–1780; Rev. W. N. Meade, Tappahannock.
Stratton Major in King and Queen, 1729–1775; Alexandria.
Truro in Fairfax, 1732–1782; Mt. Vernon.
Upper Parish in Nansemond, 1744–1793; Alexandria.
Wicomico in Northumberland, 1703–1795; Alexandria.

CHAPTER II

THREE TYPES OF PARISH EDUCATIONAL ACTIVITY

ENGLISH PRECEDENTS

There was never in England a systematic scheme of parish education but in the 16th, 17th, and 18th centuries many of the parishes as units of church and civil government participated in one way or another in the work of educating their children. The types of educational activity which have been distinguished are the establishment and support of a parish school, provision of a school building or room, the payment of tuition fees for the education of parish children in a private school, apprenticeship, administration of an endowed school, and provision of instruction in a workhouse. While the amount of activity along the lines indicated has not been exactly determined, it is evident that the colonists in America had definite precedents for public participation in education in the custom of the English parishes.[1] The fact that the English parish was transplanted to Virginia and continued without essential change naturally leads to the presumption that its educational practices were followed to a greater or less degree in the colony. A knowledge of the practice in the mother country therefore gives some direction in the attempt to discover what was done in Virginia.

In the present chapter we shall consider three types of parish educational activity—establishment and support of a school, provision of a school building, and payment for tuition of poor children in private schools—leaving for later chapters the other kinds of effort which have been mentioned.

The most common form of parish school in England in the sixteenth and the early part of the seventeenth century was that con-

---

[1] The English parish records have not been systematically examined with the purpose of determining educational practices. De Montmorency, in his *State Interference in English Education*, page 191, states a view with regard to the matter which is held by various authorities: "A systematic search of vestry records and the accounts of churchwardens and overseers would most probably show some very remarkable facts in relation to education."

ducted by the parish clerk who was then usually a clerical assistant of the minister.[2] In 1571 the Bishop of York enjoined that within his diocese,

no parish clerk be appointed against the good will of the parson. . . and that he endeavor himself to teach young children to read, if he is able so to do.[3]

Leach accepts the view expressed by a writer at the end of the seventeenth century that it was one of the understood duties of the parish clerk "to instruct children in reading and writing and rehearsing the catechism."[4]   Watson refers to Mulcaster's statement, "if the chancel have a minister the belfry hath a master,"[5] and interprets it to mean that parish clerks often acted as schoolmasters and that they sometimes used the belfry as a schoolroom.   Where it was assumed that teaching was a regular duty of the clerk he was not paid for the service, which accounts for the general lack of reference to his work in the vestry books and the wardens' accounts.   Occasionally, however, there is record of payment.   For instance the parish of St. Michael in Cornhill in 1569 paid "the clerk yt teacheth chyldren x s."[6]

Some of the parishes employed a person who had no official connection with the church to teach their children.   Occasionally in addition to the teacher a parish provided the school building or room, thus maintaining a public school in the modern sense except for the fact that the arrangements were made primarily for the poor. It was probably a more common practice, however, to hire a teacher who conducted the school in his or her own school room.   In 1636 the wardens and vestry at Cartmel ordered "That Christopher Barrow come to teach school at the ancient wages."[7]

The vestry minutes of a Westminster parish contain the following record:

Sunday, the 18th of Decr. 1681—The Peticon of Thomas Jordan praying that he may be settled and continued in the Imployment of instructing the parish Poore Children being this day read was laid aside. . . . .

In Jordan's place Judith Smith was hired,

---

[2]When in the seventeenth century it became customary to appoint laymen, often uneducated, to the position of clerk it is probable that teaching as one of the functions of the office was discontinued.

[3]Atchley, C., *The Parish Clerk*, p. 21.

[4]Leach, A. F., Article on church schools in Monroe's *Cyclopedia of Education.*

[5]*English Grammar Schools to 1660*, p. 154.

[6]Fish, C. R., "The English Parish and Education,"   *School Review*, XXIII, p. 443.

[7]Fish, above citation, p. 446.

as a fit person to undertake the Teaching of the said Poore children which was accordingly conferred upon her.[8]

The Leeds Parish vestry provided for the maintenance of a free school at the beginning of the eighteenth century.[9]   At about the same time St. Martin's-in-the-Fields set up a school in which poor children were maintained and taught.[10]   The Woolwich vestry in 1731 had under its control a schoolmaster.[11]

In numerous cases a parish provided a schoolhouse for a private teacher.   At Eltham in 1635 the parish built a school building.[12] At Ashburton in 1573 the minister paid "x s. iii d. for the occupation of the church house . . . for the keeping of scule there."[13]   The church wardens' accounts of Minchinhampton for 1651 record payment "for stones and making the chimnic in the chansell for the scoole."[14]

It seems to have been a common practice for parishes to pay for the tuition of poor children in private schools.   In 1622 the justices of Aylesham and Reipham in Norfolk County ordered,

That poore children be put to Schoole to knittinge and spinninge dames, and the churchwardens and Overseers of the poore to paie the School dames their wages, where the parents are not able.[15]

In 1628, at Dorchester, it was,

agreed that henceforth there shall be paid to the schoolmaster of the said new school founded in Holy Trinity Parish 12 d., every quarter for every poor child of the three parishes of this borough that shall be placed at school with him by the overseers of the poor . . . to be paid by the overseers every one of them for the poor of their own parish.[16]

The church wardens' accounts at Darlington for 1653 and 1655 contain the following items: "Edward Holmes a poor scholar at the *Petit* School for half-year's teaching 3 s. 3 d."; "Roger Jewett one quarter's wage for learning a boy 1/ -"; "Dame Seamer for her wages for teaching a boy one year 4/-"; "Ralph Hall for 3 lads one quarter 4/ -"; Mr. Swinburne for learning John Wilson's children and Giles' daughter's child 7/ -."[17]   The vestry of a parish in the

[8]DeMontmorency, *State Interference in English Education*, p. 191.
[9]Webb, *English Local Government*, p. 50.
[10]*Ibid.*, p. 236.
[11]*Ibid.*, p. 131.
[12]Lysons, *Environs of London*, p. 417.
[13]Fish, "The English Parish and Education," *School Review*, XXIII, 443.
[14]*Ibid.*, p. 443.
[15]Leonard, *English Poor Relief*, p. 332.
[16]Fish, p. 448.
[17]Watson, *English Grammar Schools*, p. 158.

city of Westminster in 1671 paid a school dame two shillings, six pence a week for three weeks "for teaching the parish children."[18] In the parish of Stepney, Limhouse Hamlet, in 1732 the children in the parish workhouse were "sent to a school in the Neighborhood, at the Publick charge" until eight years of age.[19]

In whatever form the educational interest of the parish in England expressed itself, the activity undertaken had as its primary purpose the provision of facilities for the instruction of the poor. It is likely, however, that in few cases were the provisions sufficient to secure the education of all the poor children in a locality.

THE PRACTICE IN VIRGINIA

PARISH READERS OR CLERKS AS TEACHERS

It was indicated in Chapter I in the discussion of parish officers and their functions that the readers or clerks who served in the Virginia parishes were laymen corresponding to the English parish clerks of the seventeenth and eighteenth centuries. It was further pointed out that they sometimes taught elementary schools. Should we understand that they taught school as a recognized part of their service to the parish, thus reflecting the earlier English practice which has been described, or that they engaged in teaching as a purely private undertaking?

There was nothing in the law defining the duties of the readers which suggests that they should conduct schools for secular instruction, and outside of the law there is little direct evidence bearing on the matter. The readers no doubt ordinarily possessed the simple qualifications required of teachers of reading and writing schools, that is, they were orthodox, they were "of good life and conversation," and they could read and write. That in the minds of the people of the time they commonly met the requirements for teachers is shown in contemporary writings. In 1696 Governor Nicholson made out a list of topics which he wanted Commissary Blair to take up with the authorities in England. One had to do with the "great scarcity of Ministers and Schoolmasters," another with the development of towns. In reference to towns and the provision of schools the following memorandum appears:

If towns go forwards that a schoolmaster be maintained in every town at

---

[18]Webb, *English Local Government*, I, p. 50.
[19]*An Account of Several Workhouses*, p. 68.

least for teaching to read English and writing. A small encouragem't to the Parish Clerk or reader may perhaps enable him to keep such a school.[20]

In Hugh Jones' account of conditions in Virginia in the first part of the eighteenth century there is a similar reference to the possession of teaching qualifications by the readers, although there is an indication that some may not have had the capacity:

In most parishes are schools (little Houses being built on Purpose) where are taught English and Writing; but to prevent the sowing of the Seeds of Dissention and Faction it is to be wished that the Masters or Mistresses should be such as are approved or licensed by the Minister and Vestry of the Parish or justices of the County, the Clerks of the Parishes being most proper for this Purpose or (in case of their incapacity or refusal) such others as can best be procured.[21]

Although the statements quoted above show sufficiently well that the readers were commonly looked upon as having the qualifications for teaching, they show that it was not a regular custom for them to engage in the work, for if it had been there would have been no occasion for the propositions made. In various writings on colonial education in Virginia, however, it is asserted that the readers taught. Bruce says that in the seventeenth century, "The readers . . . very frequently performed the duties of teachers in countryside schools."[22] Maddox says that the clerks of the parishes "were undoubtedly a main source of supply of elementary school teachers." He assumes, mistakenly, that the clerk or reader was a cleric, and says that "in the main he must have had more time and necessity to devote to teaching than had the minister himself."[23] The inference logically drawn from these and similar statements is that the readers taught school because the work naturally devolved upon them as parish servants who possessed the requisite qualifications and who had time for the work left over after caring for their regular church duties. Neither Bruce nor Maddox, however, offers any direct evidence showing that a reader ever taught. That the view implied in the statements of the authors quoted is mistaken is shown conclusively by the fact that in the vestry books there is no reference to the work of readers as teachers, and by the fact that in the reports on schools made to the Bishop of London by the ministers in 1724 there is nothing said concerning the matter.[24]

If the parish clerk was not by virtue of his office a teacher in a

[20]*Virginia Magazine of History and Biography*, VII, p. 157.
[21]Hugh Jones, *Present State of Virginia*, 1724, p. 70.
[22]Bruce, *Institutional History of Virginia*, I, p. 333.
[23]Maddox, *The Free School Idea in Virginia*, pp. 105–106.
[24]Perry, *Historical Documents*, I, pp. 262–318.

parish school, what was the relation, if any, between the functions of
clerk and teacher?   There is no direct evidence showing any customary connection in Virginia, but the practice in that colony may be
assumed to have been like that in North and South Carolina. Brickell, in his Natural History of North Carolina, written in 1737, states
in reference to church practices in the colony that "They seldom have
orthodox Clergymen," but that "The want of these Protestant clergy,
is generally supply'd by some School Masters" who serve as readers.[25]
A similar custom was sometimes followed in South Carolina.   In St.
John's Parish in that colony the settlers "had raised a Log-house 30
feet by 20, for a place of worship, and allowed their Schoolmaster a
small salary, to read for them, on Sundays, the Liturgy of the Church,
and a Sermon."[26]   In St. Mark's Parish in South Carolina the parishioners "used to meet on Sundays and have the Service of the Church
read to them by a Layman.   This duty generally devolved on the
Schoolmaster of the place."[27]   The fact seems to have been that
schoolmasters were more or less often chosen to be readers because
they had the necessary qualifications and because their work as
reader did not interfere with their regular occupation.   This statement no doubt applies as well to Virginia as to the Carolinas.[28]   It is
evident that the schools conducted by the clerks or readers were not
parish affairs.   It may be stated here that not only is there no evidence indicating that the clerks as parish servants taught school, but
there is nothing in the sources to suggest that a parish ever employed
a schoolmaster with the understanding that he was to devote his
whole time to the instruction of parish children.   That is, there were
no schools the teachers of which were supplied by the parishes.

PARISH MINISTERS AS TEACHERS

In connection with the study of the parish clerks as teachers it is
appropriate to give some consideration to the educational work of
the ministers even though it is evident that what they did does not

[25]Brickell, *Natural History of North Carolina*, p. 35.
[26]Dalcho, F., *History of the Episcopal Church in South Carolina, 1820*, p. 271.
[27]Dalcho, p. 324.
[28]Two known cases of teachers in Virginia who were readers or parish clerks are
those of Frederick Upp and William Cheeke.   Upp in 1759 was "reader in the
church on the Fork" in Augusta County.   He agreed with some of the parishioners to keep school for six months at the rate of twelve shillings and a bushel of
wheat for each child, but he was made a better offer by people in another parish
and accepted it (Stanard, *Colonial Virginia*, p. 275).   Samuel Cabell of Nelson
County went to school "in 1769, to William Cheeke, the parish clerk" (Brown,
The Cabells and Their Kin, p. 145).

come within the scope of parish educational activity.   The fact that ministers sometimes instructed boys in the better class families is brought out in various writings dealing with educational history in Virginia, the general view being that it was the common practice. W. G. McCabe in an essay on Virginia schools before the Revolution says that throughout

the whole colonial period, such education as existed was almost entirely in the hands of parsons who on their glebes, or, if unmarried, at the houses of the great land owners, conducted what were known as 'Parsons Schools.'[29]

Bruce expresses the view that the majority of the persons keeping neighborhood schools "were, throughout the seventeenth century drawn from the circle of clergymen, who thus endeavored to increase their income."[30]   In speaking of the education of John Marshall, who was taught by a young Scotch deacon, Beveridge says that the parsons "always were teachers as well as preachers."[31]

The statements concerning the educational work of the ministers in Virginia are usually generalizations based on certain well-known cases of those who, toward the end of the colonial period, prepared for college boys who later became leading men, and the source of information most commonly used is Bishop Meade's *Old Churches and Families of Virginia*.   The original sources are for the most part fragmentary in character and widely scattered, and in the absence of any official state or church records dealing with the subject main dependence has been placed in this study upon Bishop Meade's work and the biographies of eminent Virginians.

In the examination of writings which give information regarding the ministers' activity as teachers, references have been found to sixteen different pastors who taught a school or tutored in the homes of the planters.   These men may be taken up in order of the time of their service.

The first minister who served as a teacher to whom reference has been found is Rev. James Wilson who was employed in 1658 by some of the inhabitants of Elizabeth River Parish to instruct their children.[32]   No details regarding his work appear.   A letter written in 1722 tells of the employment of a young divine as tutor, probably in York County:

We have not had a schoolmaster in our neighborhood until now in five years.

---

[29]McCabe, W. Gordon, *Virginia Schools*, p. 8.
[30]Bruce, *Institutional History*, I, p. 332.
[31]Beveridge, *The Life of John Marshall*, I, p. 52.
[32]Bruce, *Institutional History*, I, p. 333.

We have now a young minister living with us who was educated at Oxford, took orders and came over as assistant to Rev. Kemp at Glocester. That parish is too poor to keep both, and he teaches for his board. He teaches Sister Susie and me, and Madam Carter's boy and two girls. . . .[33]

Mrs. Elizabeth Churchill stated in her will, drawn up in 1716, that she desired that "Mr. Bartholomew Yates undertake the instruction of my son in his own house in Latin and Greek."[34] She provided that Mr. Yates was "to be given two of the best beeves and four of the best hogs, over and above what he shall demand for teaching and board." Mr. Yates was pastor in Christ Church Parish, Middlesex County, in 1724, and he probably was in 1716.

"In 1740 Rev. James Marye opened a school in Fredericksburg to which in course of time went Washington, Madison, and Monroe.[35] The Rev. Wm. Douglas in 1748 or 1749 "came over [from Scotland] as a teacher in the family of Colonel Monroe, of Westmoreland, father of President Monroe who was one of the pupils, as was also Mr. Jefferson afterwards, in Goochland."[36]

Rev. Archibald Campbell kept a school in Westmoreland County at the middle of the eighteenth century, and "it may also be true, as tradition further reports, that General Washington and Thomas Marshall, father of the Chief-Justice, and perhaps Colonel Monroe and Mr. Madison, all of whom were born in this region, may at one time have been scholars of Mr. Campbell."[37] When John Marshall was a boy the minister in Leeds Parish, James Thompson, lived in the Marshall home for a year and taught the older children. "During his trial year the young Scotch deacon returned Thomas Marshall's hospitality by giving the elder children such instruction as occasion offered. . . ."[38] James Madison received his early training in the school of Rev. Donald Robertson, a pastor in King and Queen County:

His novitiate was passed at a school of much reputation in the County of King and Queen, conducted by an erudite Scotchman of the name of Donald Robertson. In this school he was instructed mainly in the Greek, Latin, French, and Spanish languages. . . . After leaving the school of Mr. Robertson, young Madison prosecuted his studies at home, under the tuition of the Rev. Thomas Martin, the established minister of the parish, who lived, at the time, in the family at Montpelier.[39]

---

[33]Pryor, Mrs. Roger A., *The Mother of Washington and Her Times*, p. 29.
[34]Stanard, *Colonial Virginia*, p. 276.
[35]Meade, *Old Churches*, I, p. 458.
[36]*Ibid.*, p. 458.
[37]*Ibid.*, II, p. 158.
[38]Beveridge, *Life of John Marshall*, I, p. 52.
[39]Rives, *Life of Madison*, p. 10

As will be shown later, the minister of Elizabeth River Parish in Norfolk County in 1762, Alexander Rhonnald, had been previously master of a charity school in a neighboring county. The school was very probably the Eaton School, an endowed institution which will be considered in the following chapter.

Rev. Jonathan Boucher, who is perhaps the best known of the Virginia colonial schoolmasters, conducted a boarding school first in Hanover Parish and then in St. Mary's Parish from 1762 until 1774. He says in a letter to Washington, who placed his step-son in the school,

I had now also increased my number of boys to nearly thirty, most of them the sons of the first condition in the colony. They all boarded with me, and I wholly superintended them myself, without any usher, for two years.[40]

Nicholas Cabell attended the,

classical school of Rev. James Maury of Albemarle, of the Parson's Cause fame from May, 1767, to May 1769, in which year Mr. Maury died. Thomas Jefferson Bishop Madison, John Taylor or Carolina, Dabney Carr, the elder, and numerous other distinguished men were educated by Mr. Maury.[41]

Another dominie noted for his inspiring use of the rod, was the Rev. John Cameron, D.D., a graduate of King's College, Aberdeen, who came over to Virginia from Scotland in 1770, and long taught a select classical school in Lunenburg County, where he was also minister of the parish.[42]

In 1771 a young minister who was seeking appointment to a parish advertised in the Williamsburg *Gazette* that he intended to teach school as well as serve as pastor, and he probably carried out his intention.

To the Publick:—A clergyman of the Church of England, a sober young man, with a good character, would serve as a minister to a Church in any of his Majesty's Plantations, upon Trial, on reasonable terms. He proposes to teach Ladies and Gentlemen the French, Latin, Greek, and English Languages, Book-keeping by double entry, Algebra, Geometry, surveying, Mechanicks, Fortification, Gunnery, Navigation, and the use of the Globes and Maps, after a natural, easy, and concise method, without Burthen to the Memory. For particulars, Letters directed (postpaid), to the Reverend W. S., to the care of the Reverend Thomas Smith, Rector of Cople Parish in Westmoreland, Potowmack, Virginia, will have proper answers as soon as possible.[43]

The diary of Col. William Cabell contains the following entry for November 7, 1775:

---

[40]*Letters from Jonathan Boucher to George Washington*, p. 5.
[41]Brown, Alexander, *The Cabells and Their Kin*, p. 145.
[42]McCabe, W. G., *Virginia Schools*, pp. 11–12.
[43]*William and Mary College Quarterly*, VII, p. 178.

The Rev. Robert Buchan began his school at my house, and all my children are put under his tuition.[44]

Bishop Meade quotes a statement that the Rev. James Maury Fontaine kept a school when he was minister in Ware Parish.[45]

The above completes the list of ministers who taught school of whose work record has been found. Doubtless there were others and we are justified in concluding that the practice was fairly common. There are various facts, however, the consideration of which shows that the custom was not universal. Bishop Meade had a comprehensive acquaintance with the possible sources of information concerning the colonial ministers' work, and he undoubtedly would have found others among them who taught if in fact the larger share of them followed the practice. The clergy in Virginia petitioned Governor Andros in 1695 for an increase in their salaries, and the petition was sent on to the Burgesses, who refused to comply with the request because they thought the salaries then paid were sufficient, considering the fact that the ministers also received certain perquisites. The ministers' reply contained the following statement:

As to our considerable Perquisites, wee beg leave to inform your Excell'y that wee have noe Perquisites but for marriages and a few funeral Sermons, and that by a computation wee have made of the Perquisites of the generality of our Parishes, wee find that they do not amount communibus Annis to above five pounds per annum.[46]

If it had been the regular custom at the time for the ministers to teach school, there probably would have been some reference to this work as a source of income. Neither Robert Beverley nor Hugh Jones in their accounts of conditions in the colony at the beginning of the eighteenth century make reference to the work of ministers as teachers, although they give particular attention to education. In 1724 the Bishop of London sent to the ministers in Virginia a set of questions inquiring about conditions and practices in the parishes, to which twenty-nine replied.[47] In response to the question concerning education no one made reference to his teaching school although private schools are mentioned. It is likely that, as the above statements concerning individual pastors suggest, it was more common toward the end of the colonial period for the ministers to act as teachers or tutors than it had been previously. The general

---

[44]Brown, *The Cabells and Their Kin*, p. 191.
[45]Meade, *Old Churches*, I, p. 328.
[46]Anderson, J. S. M., *History of the Colonial Church*, I, p. 603.
[47]Perry, *Historical Collections*, I, pp. 262–318.

advance of culture and the growth in importance of William and Mary College were factors creating a demand for the Latin instruction which the ministers could give.

PAYMENT BY THE PARISH FOR THE INSTRUCTION OF POOR CHILDREN

Although it seems to have been a fairly common custom in England to make expenditures out of parish funds for the education of poor children in private schools, the parishes in Virginia did not adopt the practice. An examination of practically all of the extant vestry books shows only five cases. The minutes of the meeting of the Petsworth Parish vestry in October, 1713, contain the following entry:

Dr. to Ezekiell Smith for keeping and schooling Jane Halloway — 800
to Wm. Anderson for keeping and schooling Mary Launlings—500.[48]

The figures given indicate the number of pounds of tobacco paid. In 1744 the vestry of Fredericksville Parish in Louisa County paid Richard Farmer eight pounds and ten shillings for providing for the support of a girl until she should become eighteen years of age and for giving her "two years schooling to learn it to read." The Albemarle Parish vestry in 1748 "Ordered that the Church Wardens do pay out of the Fines in Their Hands for one Year's Schooling of a child of a certain Frances Copeland, a Woman under Low Circumstances."[49] In 1771 the vestry of Wicomico Parish paid for the instruction of a poor child.[50]

The small number of cases where expenditure was made for the education of poor children makes it impossible to attach any positive significance to the action taken except that it shows that the vestries thought they possessed the right, possibly because of English custom, to make outlay for the education of individual children. If it had seemed desirable to the local governments, a general practice of educating poor childern in private school at parish expense could have developed.

PARISH PROVISION OF SCHOOL BUILDING

It was not the custom for the parishes of colonial Virginia to provide schoolhouses for the free use of masters to induce them to conduct schools. The only case found is mentioned in the record of Linhaven Parish in Princess Anne County. In the minutes of the

[48]MS. copy of Petsworth vestry book, p. 86.
[49]Albemarle Parish MS. vestry book, April 12, 1748.
[50]Wicomico Parish vestry book, p. 57.

vestry meeting in this parish held March 2, 1736 the following entry appears:

On the motion of Col. Anthony Walke that the old Church woo'd be a convenient place to make a public school off for instructing children to learning, that liberty might be given for ye applying it to that purpose, ye vestry taking the said proposall also being of the opinion that after it is made commodious 'twould be an encouragement to induce a master constantly to attend thereon; Do therefore unanimously Resolve that ye said Church be, and it is hereby given for the use aforesaid, and to and for no other use or purpose whatsoever.[51]

The vestry of Elizabeth River Parish in Norfolk County allowed Mr. James Pasteur to take the bricks and timber of the old church to build a house, presumably a schoolhouse, on the "school land."[52] The land had probably been given to the parish for school purposes.

It is clear that with negligible exceptions the parishes in colonial Virginia did not aid in the education of their children by establishing schools, by paying for instruction in private schools, or by furnishing community school buildings. We shall next consider the endowed type of parish school the operation of which did not require public expenditure.[53]

[51]MS. Vestry Minutes of Linhaven Parish, March 2, 1736. A similar case except that the court took the action is found in the records of Essex County:
At a Court held for Essex Co. Feb. 10, 1704. On the motion of Capt. Robert Coleman, It is considered by the Court that the Old Prison standing at Hobses Hole Tappahannock be appropriated to the use of a Schoole house, and to no other use whatsoever. (Essex County, Order Book, 1703–08, p. 147).
At a Court held for Essex August 1705. The Petition of Richard Cooke Keeper of the School at Hobbs Hole to have liberty to live in the sd School house is Referd to the consideration of the next Court. (*William and Mary College Quarterly*, Ser. 2, I, p. 142, contributed by Clayton Torrence).
[52]Meade, *Old Churches*, I, 276.
[53]The following note concerning educational provisions among the German and French settlers in Virginia may be added here.
In the German settlement at Germanna, in Orange County, a school was established shortly after 1739 of which the pastor was the regular teacher. The Germans here were allowed to have their own religious parish organization separate from the official parish. The facts concerning the school are given by Schuricht, in his *German Element in Virginia*, page 75:
In 1739 Rev. Stoever travelled to Germany in order to raise money for building a church, a parsonage with schoolrooms, and to establish a library. The instruction in school afterwards was given by the venerable parson himself and it comprised religion, reading, writing, and arithmetic.
In Rockingham County in 1769 a parish school was established by the Germans worshipping at the Peaked Mountain Church, but the minister here was apparently not the teacher. The arrangement under which the school was operated as indicated in the following statement is of interest.
"Agreement between the Reformed and Lutheran Congregations Worshipping in the Peaked Mountain Church; Rockingham County, Virginia, October 31, 1769
We have established it as a union church, in the use of which the Lutherans and their descendants as well as the Reformed and their descendants, shall have equal share. But since it is necessary to keep in repair the church and the schoolhouse

and support the minister and schoolmaster, therefore, we have drawn up this writing that each member sign his name to the same and thereby certify that he will support the minister and schoolmaster and help to keep in repair the church and schoolhouse as far as lies in his ability. Should, however, one or another withdraw himself from such Christian work (which we would not suppose a Christian would do), we have unitedly concluded that such a one shall not be looked upon as a member of our congregation."

As a penalty for failure to help in support of the church and school it was agreed that those who should withdraw themselves from the work should pay for a baptism two shillings, six pence, and for communion or confirmation five shillings (Wayland, *A History of Rockingham County*, Virginia, p. 61).

At the beginning of the eighteenth century French Huguenots made a settlement in King William Parish on the south side of the James River in what was then Henrico County. The parish government was in their hands and the record was kept in French until 1750. The activity of the parish government as shown in the vestry record was essentially like that in other parishes, except that there is no indication that the vestry and wardens bound out children as apprentices. What they did with reference to schools has not been determined. The only allusion to schools in King William Parish which has been found in the course of this study is that made by Bishop Meade. He says,

"Even the little establishment of Huguenots at Manakintown, whose compact settlement so favoured education, and whose parentage made its members to desire it, was so destitute, that about this time (1724) one of their leading men, a Mr. Sallie, on hearing that the King was about to establish a colony in Ireland for the Huguenots, addressed him a letter begging permission to be united to it, saying that there was no school among them where their children could be educated" (Meade, *Old Churches*, I, p. 190).

CHAPTER III

ENDOWED PARISH SCHOOLS

ENGLISH PRECEDENTS

In the reign of Elizabeth a number of free elementary schools were established in England by gifts similar to those upon which the grammar schools were founded, and in the seventeenth century endowed schools of this type became common.[1]   Between 1660 and 1730 no less than 905 non-classical endowed schools were set up.   Some and probably many of these institutions were parish schools, that is, the founders either gave them directly to the parishes or provided that the wardens or vestry should administer them for the good of parish children.   For instance, in St. Olave's Parish in Southwark in 1561 the church wardens were ordered to receive moneys from the executors of an estate to set up a free school and choose a schoolmaster to teach children to write, read, and cast accounts.[2]

Whatever is the general explanation of the great interest in the education of the poor which was shown in England by the many gifts for the founding of schools, no doubt in the colonies the same interest was felt; and where there was no development of common public schools or of church schools which provided for the poor we should expect to find that benevolent men followed the English custom and established free schools by endowment.   It is well known that in fact there were in colonial Virginia, as in the other southern colonies, a number of such institutions and that some were in control of the parishes.   It is the purpose in the present chapter to determine the number, character, and service of the endowed parish schools in Virginia, and as far as may be to ascertain what share they constituted of all the endowed schools in the colony.

---

[1] De Montmorency, *State Interference in English Education*, pp. 189–90; statement based on the Digest of Schools and Charities for Education reported to Parliament in 1842.

[2] Watson, *English Grammar Schools*, p. 150.

ENDOWED PARISH SCHOOLS IN VIRGINIA

The official records from which information concerning the endowed parish schools of colonial Virginia may be gained are the minutes of the vestry meetings, the county court records, the Acts of the Assembly, and the reports on educational conditions in 1724 which were made to the Bishop of London whose diocese embraced the colonies. The number of extant vestry books, the period they cover, and the character of their contents have been indicated. In the colonial statutes are found several Acts of incorporation which give the essential provisions in the wills of the founders of certain schools and show something of the operation of the institutions. The court records of wills and orders give evidence regarding bequests and the management of schools. With small exception the voluminous court records have not been printed, and only those in print and the published extracts dealing with schools have been used in the course of the present study. The reports of 1724, although brief, are the best contemporary source of information concerning schools as a whole in the colony at any one time, and in a number of instances they help in interpreting data relating to those established in the years before the survey was made. They also furnish a means of checking up on material found in other sources. The contemporary writings of an unofficial type which refer to endowed schools in the colony are few and they add but little to the facts supplied by the public records. Because of the bearing of the facts in the reports of 1724 on the period preceding that year rather than on that which follows, consideration will first be given to the schools founded in the earlier period.

ENDOWED PARISH SCHOOLS ESTABLISHED BEFORE 1724

The question asked of the parish ministers in Virginia by the Bishop of London was,

Have you in your Parish any Public School for the instruction of youth? If you have, is it endowed? and who is the Master?[3]

[3]Perry, W. S., *Historical Collections Relating to the American Colonial Church*, I, p. 261.   The inquiry of the Bishop embraced questions concerning religious and social conditions in the colony, so that for each of the 29 parishes from which replies were received there is a fairly good description of the situation.   The same survey was made in Maryland and Connecticut.   The parishes in Virginia which were reported upon were the following: Westminster (location undetermined), St. Paul's in Hanover County, James City in James City County, Bristol in Prince George, St. Peter's in New Kent, Westover in Charles City, Hungars in Northampton, Newport in Isle of Wight, Stratton Major in King and Queen, Wilmington (location undetermined), Blissland in New Kent, York Hampton in

A typical reply from a parish where there was no public school is the following from St. Peter's Parish in New Kent County:

We have no Public Schools but some private, wherein children are taught to read, write, etc.[4]

The Bishop's inquiry does not indicate what he meant by "public school," but it is evident that the ministers understood the term to signify simply a school which was not operated privately for gain, and in effect this meant a school open without charge to at least some of the children of the community in which it was located, with support coming from endowment, occasional gifts, or taxation.[5] That is, the term was an inclusive one under which the ministers might list any kind of free school; in fact, however, all the public schools reported in 1724 were endowed. In taking up the endowed parish schools we may consider separately each parish in which one was reported.

Elizabeth City Parish in Elizabeth City County

The minister of Elizabeth City Parish reported in 1724 that in his parish,

There are two schools endowed, though very meanly, whereof John Mason and Abram Paris are teachers. There is also a very good private school where, besides reading, arithmetic and writing, Latin and Greek are very well taught, whereof William Fyfe, a man of good life and conversation is master.[6]

The endowed schools referred to were two which had been founded in the seventeenth century upon the bequests of Benjamin Syms and Thomas Eaton. The earliest reference to the Syms School, which

---

York, Christ Church in Lancaster, South Farnham in Essex, Petsworth in Gloucester, Lawn's Creek in Surry, Washington in Westmoreland, Elizabeth City in Elizabeth City, Upper Parish in Isle of Wight, Christ Church in Middlesex, Bruton in James City, Accomako in Accomac, St. Stephen's in King and Queen, Henrico in Henrico, Southwark in Surry, Abingdon in Gloucester, St. Mary's in Essex, Overwharton in Stafford, St. Anne's in Essex.

[4]*Ibid.*, p. 269.

[5]While it is clear that the ministers in 1724 all agreed in their understanding of "public school" as meaning a free school, the term was sometimes used in the later colonial period, at least, in application to a purely private institution operated for profit and public only in the sense that public patronage was desired. An illustration of this use is found in the following advertisement appearing in the *Williamsburg Gazette* in 1771:

"John Bruce, M. A., has opened a Publick School over against the Church, at the head of Cumberland Street, Norfolk, and proposes to teach the Greek, Latin, and English Languages, Navigation, Bookkeeping, Arithmetick, Mathematicks; where those who choose to favor him with the Instruction of their Children, may depend on all due attention being paid their education." (Quoted in *William and Mary College Quarterly*, VII, p. 178).

[6]Perry, W. S., *Historical Collections*, I, p. 294.

was established first, is in an Act of 1642-43[7] confirming the donor's will which was drawn up in 1634-35.[8] Syms provided that two hundred acres of land in the county and parish of Elizabeth City which he owned, together with the milk and increase of eight milch cows, should be given,

for the maintenance of a learned, honest man, to keep upon the said ground a free school for the education and instruction of the children of the adjoining parishes of Elizabeth City and Kiquotan

The will further declared it to be the desire of Syms,

that the justices of the peace of the said county of Elizabeth City, with the minister and churchwardens of the said parish of Elizabeth City, should see his will justly and truly performed, and further declared his will to be, that when there should be a sufficient increase of the said cattle, part of them should be sold, and the money raised by such sale, laid out in building a schoolhouse, and that the residue of the said increase, after the schoolmaster should have a sufficient stock, should be applied towards repairing the said house, and maintaining poor children, or decayed or maimed persons.[9]

It appears from the fact that the will was confirmed in 1642-43 that Syms had died shortly before, so that the date of his bequest may be set as early as 1641.[10] The sanctioning of the will in 1642-43 made the property available at that time, and probably the school was put in operation shortly thereafter. It was certainly running before 1647, for the author of *A Perfect Description of Virginia*, which was written in that year, said in reference to it,

I may not forget to tell you we have a Free-School, with two hundred Acres of Land, a fine house upon it, forty milch Kine, and other accommodations to it: the Benefactor deserves perpetual memory: His name Mr. Benjamin Symes, worthy to be Chronicled, other petty schools also we have.[11]

The school is again referred to in a court record of 1693 which shows that it was then in operation, as presumably it had been in the preceding years, and that the schoolhouse was kept up. It was ordered that,

Robert Crook Schoolmaster of Symmes School be allowed and paid for his charges in repairing ye school House two old cows in lieu thereof.[12]

---

[7]Hening, I, p. 252.

[8]The will is apparently not in existence, but its date and terms are given in an Act incorporating its trustees passed in 1753 (Hening, VI, p. 389).

[9]Hening, VI, p. 389

[10]Syms was apparently the first man to provide in his will for the endowment of an American school, but the bequest made upon his death was antedated by that of John Harvard by three years.

[11]*A Perfect Description of Virginia*, Force Historical Tracts, II, p. 16.

[12]Quoted by Lyon G. Tyler in *William and Mary College Quarterly*, VI, p. 74. The court records of Elizabeth City County for the years previous to 1689 are not in existence. While in the early years of the existence of the Syms School there was a schoolhouse separate from the dwelling, it seems that at the middle of the

The court record shows that in 1699 Crook resigned and that a new master was appointed. The next reference to the Syms School which has been found appears in an advertisement in the *Williamsburg Gazette* of March 12, 1752:

Notice is hereby given, that Symmes' Free School, in Elizabeth City County, will be vacant on the 25th of March, a tutor of a good character, and properly qualified may meet with good encouragement by applying to the Trustees of the Said School.

N. B.   The Land Rent of the said School is 31£ per Ann., besides Perquisites.[13]

At this time, and possibly long before, it was the custom to rent the Syms farm, reserving only the plot on which was located the master's dwelling in which the school was kept. When the farm was leased in 1760 "one acre at the southwest corner"[14] with buildings was reserved, and apparently this was the location of the school.

In 1753 the trustees of the school were incorporated by the Assembly with the intention, indicated in the act of incorporation, of

enabling the justices of the peace of the county of Elizabeth City, and the minister and churchwardens of the parish of Elizabeth City, in that county, to take and hold certain lands devised by the will of Benjamin Sym, for a free school, and other charitable uses.[15]

After giving the terms of Syms' will the Act goes on to state that "the charitable intentions of the said Benjamin Sym, the donor, hath not been effectually fulfilled," and that it was the desire of the Assembly to incorporate the trustees "to the end that the said charity may be more beneficial for the future." In just what way Syms' intentions had not been carried out is not stated, but the Act implies that lessees were in arrears of rents, that damages had been "sustained by occasion of not repairing the houses" on the land, and that the master of the school may have assumed a vested right

---

eighteenth century at least the school was kept in the master's dwelling. Section IV of an Act of 1753, incorporating the trustees, provides that they should use the rents in part for the purpose of "erecting and keeping in repair a sufficient schoolhouse for his [the master's] dwelling." (Hening, VI, pp. 389–92).

[13]A bound volume containing the issues of the *Williamsburg Gazette* for 1752 is in the New York Public Library. The perquisites referred to in the advertisement, as suggested in a rental contract made in 1760, consisted in the use of four cows and the combined school building and dwelling. The use and increase of the cattle belonging to the school were given with the land, the schoolmaster after 1760 having the use of four cows which were pastured for him. In 1760 the school herd consisted of "eleven head of black cattle" (*The Syms-Eaton Free School*, p. 14).

[14]From an indenture appearing in Elizabeth City County records, quoted in *The Syms-Eaton Free School*, pp. 13–15.

[15]Hening, VI, 390.

in his position without control by the trustees.   The Act allowed the trustees,

to nominate and appoint when, and often as they shall think good, such persons as they shall approve of, to be master of the said free school. . . .And the said trustees and the Governors, and their successors for the time being, shall and may have full power and authority to visit the said free school, and to order, reform, and redress all disorder and abuses in and touching the government and disposing of the same, and to remove the said master, as to them, or the greater part of them, shall seem just, fit, and convenient.

It seems probable that the trustees in the preceding period of the school's history had exercised little oversight, so that a precedent had grown up which made it necessary for those in charge of the school in 1753 to ask for legislative action in order that they might regain control.   The inaction of the trustees is indicated by the lack of records showing regulation from 1699 to 1752.   While the title of the Act of incorporation suggests that the chief end sought by incorporation was the delegation of the right to control the school lands, the fact that the rental in 1760,[16] seven years after the incorporation, was the same as in 1752, as shown by the advertisement quoted above, indicates that the main purpose was to allow the trustees to regain control of the management of the school and perhaps to make clear their responsibility in the matter.   In any case it is evident that for a considerable period the school was not carefully managed.

After 1753 there is no reference to the Syms School in the sources examined except in the lease of 1760 referred to, but there is no reason for thinking that it was not in continuous operation during the remainder of the colonial period.   Considering the long period during which the school was in existence, the data giving information concerning it are relatively few, and we can tell little directly from the records with regard to its real character.   It is evident, however, that it was a free endowed school controlled by a board of trustees composed of county and parish officials, the participation of parish officers making it appropriate to consider it as one among a number of institutions of a similar general type which were purely parish affairs.

Besides the Syms School there was in Elizabeth City Parish in 1724 another endowed institution known as the Eaton Free School, which was founded on the bequest of Thomas Eaton in compliance

---

[16]Rental indenture, county clerk's office, quoted in *The Syms-Eaton Free School*, pp. 13–14.

with his will drawn up in 1659.   This was one of the two endowed schools to which the minister of the parish referred.   The character of Eaton's gift and his intention with reference to its use are shown in the following extract from the will.

I have for the maintenance of an able Schoolmaster to educate and teach the children borne within the said county of Elizabeth City. . . .

Given, granted, assigned, set over and confirmed and doo by these presents give, grant, assign, set over and confirm after the time of my decease for the use aforesaid, Five hundred acres of land, whereon the said Free School shall be kept, . . . Two negroes . . . Twelve Cows and two Bulls, Twenty hogs, [here is given a list of household utensils as a part of the grant] to have and to hould the said land with all other the premises before mentioned for the use afores'd, with all ye male increase thereof, for ye maintenance of the said schoolmaster such one as by the Commissioners, Mynister & churchwardens whom I doo nominate and appoint as trustees in trust for the ordering and settling thereof from time to time shall be thought fit, and I, the said Thomas Eaton do further order and appoint that no free education bee allowed but to such children as shall be borne within the said county.[17]

The Eaton School was in all likelihood opened shortly subsequent to the donor's death, which probably occurred not long after 1659. It was certainly in operation some time before 1692, for in that year the court record shows that the trustees required that a man who had served as master previous to that time should provide food and clothing for an old slave given in the bequest whom he had neglected to care for properly:

Whereas Mr. Ebenezer Taylor, late schoolmaster of Eaton's free-school, his time being expired & having had ye Benefitt and p'quisetts thereof, It is thought reasonable yt a negroe woman belonging to ye sd schoole should be cloathed at ye charges of ye sd schoolemaster. . . .[18]

There are brief references to the Eaton School in the court records for 1693 and 1695.   The record for 1697, showing the appointment of a teacher, indicates that instruction was given at that time in "gramer learninge" as well as in English:

Mr. George Eland with consent of this court is elected Schoolmaster of Eaton's free school & he is to continue in place as he shall be approved of from year to year Teaching all such children in English and gramer learninge as shall be sent to him yt are belonging to this county, and he is to have all such p'quisettes and p'fitts as is belonging to ye s'd schoole.[19]

In 1699 part of the Eaton farm was rented for a period of twenty-one years, the lessee agreeing to pay two hundred pounds of tobacco

---

[17]*William and Mary College Quarterly*, XI, pp. 19–20.
[18]*Ibid.*, p. 74.   The earliest record book of Elizabeth City County begins with the year 1689.
[19]*Ibid.*, p. 74.

per year, plant one hundred apple trees, and build, apparently for the master, "one substantial thirty-foot dwelling house."[20] The land had been leased some time previous to 1699 which makes it appear that from an early date it was the custom to rent the farm, the master receiving the income and the use of the dwelling and schoolhouse.

The record for 1720 contains the following statement showing that the Elizabeth City Parish vestry had taken a part in controlling the school property even though according to the terms of the will it had no right in the matter:

Upon compl't made by Henry Irvin gent ag't Jno Curle about Eaton's free schoole land of waste being made of the timbers, it is ordered that the Clk, bring s'd Eaton's will and Deed to next court concerning the premises and a copy of the vestry ord'r whereby Curle hath the land granted to him.[21]

In 1725 the school land was rented with the understanding that in return for the use of the property the lessee should provide a schoolmaster, thus relieving the trustees of their responsibility:

Upon the motion of William Tucker setting forth that he is willing to take the school land and provide a schoolmaster, it is ordered that the said Tucker have possession of the said land with this proviso and condition, that he constantly keep and provide a schoolmaster to teach children in said land.[22]

The extracts from the records of 1720 and 1725 given above suggest that the trustees were not exercising proper care in managing the school and its property. As a means of eliminating any doubt about their power and obligation the Assembly in 1730 passed an Act allowing them "to take and hold certain lands given by Thomas Eaton to charitable uses and to lett leases thereof."[23]

Notwithstanding the passage of the Act of 1730 the management of the Eaton property did not improve, as is shown in an Act of incorporation enacted in 1759 entitled "An Act for the better regulating Eaton's Charity School."[24] In the Act it is stated or directly implied that part of the lands had not been profitable "the trustees having neglected to let the same," that "some of the leases were either lost or in the custody of the tenants who would not produce them," that waste had been committed on the lands without the recovery of damages, and that there had been breach of contract by the lessees in not building and planting on the farm according to the

---

[20]Court record, June 19, 1699. Quoted in *The Syms-Eaton Free School*, p. 11.
[21]*William and Mary College Quarterly*, VI, p. 74.
[22]Court record, Nov. 17, 1725. Quoted in *The Syms-Eaton Free School*, p. 11.
[23]Hening, VII, pp. 317–18.
[24]Hening, VII, pp. 317–19.

terms of the leases. A partial explanation of the inaction of the
trustees, according to a statement in the Act, lay in the fact that
they doubted their authority, although this could not explain neg-
ligence in renting the land or loss of the leases, and in view of the
provisions of the Eaton will and the Act of 1730 it does not seem that
it could have been the real reason for failure to act in the cases of the
other matters mentioned. The real explanation for the facts indicated seems to have been quite clearly that the trustees for a long
period neglected their trust so that abuses grew up. If in fact the
trustees had looked upon their lack of power as the reason for inaction
they could have asked for and secured their incorporation long before
1759.

The Eaton School trustees not only were negligent in the management of the school land, but, as is shown in the following excerpt from
the Act of incorporation, they were careless in at least one important
particular in carrying out their duty in the management of the schoo.

And whereas the said foundation hath been abused, by admitting a great
number of children into the said school, whose parents are well able to pay for
their education: For remedy whereof, Be it enacted by *the authority aforesaid*,
That no person shall enjoy the benefit of the said charity-school without the consent of the master, for the time being except such poor children as the said trustees
and governors and their successors, or the greater part of them, shall from time
to time declare to be the proper objects of the pious founder's charity.[25]

The above paragraph suggests that the trustees had allowed the
children of the well-to-do to attend the school and that they had
either excluded the poor for whom it was founded or had allowed a
custom to grow up which kept them out. There is evidence in the
following quotation from a letter written in 1762 by the pastor of
Elizabeth River Parish in Norfolk County pointing to the conclusion
that the trustees were directly responsible for the abuse.

I had a charity school in a neighboring county where the Gentlemen's children
were many years educated, and the objects of charity disdained, till I was obliged
to leave the school, and lodge a Complaint in the Assembly, which has pre-
vented the Grandees to reign longer, but from that time, they use me with the
most invidious Terms of Ill nature for my pains.[26]

While the extract from the letter does not absolutely establish
the fact that the minister who wrote it was referring to the Eaton
School, a comparison between it and the paragraph from the Act
quoted above makes it seem fairly certain that such was the case.

---

[25]Hening, VII, p. 320.
[26]Letter of Alexander Rhonnald to Rev. Dr. John Waring, Sept. 27, 1762;
Bray MS., Box II, Minute Book B, p. 189. Found by W. W. Kemp.

The county in which the Eaton School was located was "a neighboring county," and there is no reference in the statutes to a legislative attempt to correct an abuse of the kind indicated except in the case of the Eaton School. Evidently when the minister who wrote the letter was master of the school he had endeavored without success to get the trustees to admit the poor so that he had to appeal to the Assembly. The Act no doubt restored the school to its original purpose, although it apparently allowed the master to take in some of the better class in cases where they obtained his consent.

There seems to be no further reference to the Eaton School or the official records until after the end of the colonial period except in an entry in the Elizabeth City Parish vestry book of 1772 showing parish indebtedness in an amount the record of which is obliterated "To the Trustees of Eaton's Free School for 3 years rent of 10 acres Land for the use of the Poor House."[27]

The extracts from the records which have been given show that the Eaton School was a parish-county institution similar to the one founded by Syms. The county record in which the action of the Trustees was entered gives no indication that the Elizabeth City Parish minister and church wardens had a part in managing the school but there is no doubt that they acted with the justices in accordance with the terms of the will. In fact it seems that upon one occasion at least the vestry exercised some control, for the record of 1720 indicates that they had orderd the renting of part of the school land. It is clear that throughout its more than a century of existence the Eaton School had an income from its original endowment sufficient to provide a master. The exact amount received at any time is nowhere stated, but the fact that a man who leased the farm in 1725 was required only to supply a master as payment and that the Syms School trustees were able to get a master for thirty pounds a year suggests that the income was approximately the same as in the case of the Syms School.

Abingdon and Ware Parishes in Gloucester County

The answer made by the minister of Abingdon Parish to the nquiry of the Bishop of London concerning schools in his parish in 1724 was as follows:

A free School endowed with 500 acres of good land, 3 slaves, cattle & household goods. The Master is George Ransom a native of Virginia.[28]

[27]Elizabeth City Parish vestry book, p. 139.
[28]Perry, *Historical Collections*, I, p. 309.

The school referred to was undoubtedly one provided for in the
will of Henry Peasley which was drawn up in 1675. The will is not
in existence but a summary of it appears in an Act of 1756 incorporating the trustees. The Act[29] stated that in 1675 Peasley devised,

a tract or parcel of land, containing six hundred acres, or thereabouts, lying in and
being in the Parish of Abingdon, . . . together with ten cows and one breeding
mare, for the maintenance of a free school forever, to be kept with a schoolmaster for the education of children of the Parishes of Abingdon and Ware,
forever.

The occasion for action by the Assembly in 1756 is shown in the
second and third paragraphs of the Act:

And whereas several slaves have been by different persons, since the above
devise, given for the same purposes, but, by reason of the inconvenient situation
of the said land, few children frequent the free school kept there, so that the
charitable intention of the said Henry Peasley, and the other donors, is of little
benefit to the said two parishes.

And whereas it is represented to this present General Assembly, by the
ministers, church wardens, and vestrymen of the said two parishes of Abingdon
and Ware, that if proper persons were impowered to lease out the said land and
slaves, the annual rents thereof would be sufficient to support and maintain a free
school in each of the said parishes for the education of the children residing
there. . . .

The Act then goes on to provide for the incorporation of the
officers mentioned and to require them "to erect and found a free
school in some convenient part of each of the said parishes of Abingdon and Ware." The arrangement was clearly in harmony with
the intention of Peasley.

The above quotations show that up to 1756 the Peasley School
was in Abingdon Parish, and the presumption is that it belonged to
the two parishes mentioned in the Act and was controlled by their
officers. The date of the will suggests that the school was in operation some time before the end of the seventeenth century, but the
loss of the vestry records of the parishes concerned and the lack of
other data except those contained in the Act of 1756 and the minister's
report make it impossible to determine much about it. The clause
"if proper persons were impowered to lease out the said land and
slaves," suggests that up to 1756 the trustees had acted on the assumption that they did not have the power to lease the property and that
probably the master of the school had had its use as his compensation.
It is difficult to understand why the action taken in 1756 was not
taken long before that date, for no doubt the location of the Peasley

[29]Hening, VII, pp. 41–43.

School had been unfavorable from the first. Whether the two parish schools were established in accordance with the direction of the Assembly cannot be determined with certainty, but it is unlikely that the officers of the two parishes would have requested power to make the arrangement if they had not desired and intended to use the permission given. It is reasonably certain that the school was in continuous operation from the latter part of the seventeenth century until 1756, and we may assume that after that year there was a school supported mainly from the income of the Peasley bequest in each of the parishes mentioned. Probably the old school in Abingdon Parish was moved to a more satisfactory location than it had had before 1756.[30]

Accomac Parish in Accomac County

In 1724 it was reported from Accomac Parish that there was in the parish,

a school endowed by one Mr. Sandford, late of London. John Moragh, an Irish man, is at present Master of it.[31]

Sandford had formerly lived in Accomac, but his will was drawn up in London and proved there in 1710.[32] The endowment was given

for the benefit, better learning, and education of poor children, whose parents are esteemed unable to give them learning, living in the upper part of Accomack county, in Virginia.[33]

The property, the rents and profits of which went to the school, consisted of three tracts of land containing 3420 acres. The management of the school was placed in the hands of the county commissioners living in Accomac Parish, the church wardens, and the vestry.[34] Probably the school was opened within a year or two after 1710 and continued in operation, although no facts concerning the school itself except those given by the minister as stated above have been found.

---

[30]No attempt has here been made to determine what was done with the Peasley school or property after the colonial period, but it appears from a statement in *Colonial Churches of Virginia* made by Rev. W. B. Lee, the rector of Abingdon Parish in 1908, that "some years ago this bequest was changed by the Virginia Legislature to benefit the poor of Gloucester county." The rector also speaks of a parishioner, Mr. Joe Deal, who "owned a part of the Free School Tract, and lived and died in the original Peasley house, built about 1655" (*Colonial Churches of Virginia*, pp. 185, 187).

[31]Perry, *Historical Collections*, I, p. 302.

[32]*Virginia Magazine of History*, XVIII, p. 180.

[33]Meade, *Old Churches and Families of Virginia*, I, p. 265.

[34]*Ibid.*, p. 265.

Washington Parish in Westmoreland County

The minister of Washington Parish reported in 1724 as follows:

The gentleman who bequeathed my Glebe to the parish left the whole tract (containing 440 acres), to be disposed of by the Vestry for the better maintenance of a minister and schoolmaster, the Vestry made no division of the land, but gave it to me as a glebe, with this proviso, that I provide a sufficient person to instruct the youth in reading, writing and arithmetic under my inspection, which condition I have complied with.[35]

The minister's report does not indicate who made the gift to the parish, but Tyler states that the donor was William Horton,[36] who, as shown in the county records, made a bequest to Washington Parish in a will drawn up in 1700. Very probably the school was started shortly after the donor's death, but the statement by the minister, Lawrence DeButts, that "the Vestry made no division of the land, but gave it to me as a glebe" suggests that he may have been the first minister in the parish who had had the use of the land and that the school was not opened until after his incumbency began. DeButts left England some time after July, 1721.[37] The vestry record of Washington Parish is not in existence and no facts concerning the Horton School except those given above appear. We may assume, however, that the school was kept in operation after 1721 at least, even though it probably was necessary to allow the master to take in pay pupils. The conduct of the school by the parish minister would have met the requirements of the will, and it may be that this was the arrangement sometimes made.

St. Stephen's Parish in Northumberland County

It seems probable that in addition to the five parish free schools established before 1724 there was one other school in operation for a time at least which was not in charge of parish officials. While the school did not belong to the parish in which it was located we may consider it here because it apparently completes the list of endowed schools in operation before 1724, and because the will which provided for it supplies information which aids in determining facts in regard to the character of the other schools which have been mentioned. The office of minister in St. Stephen's Parish[38] was vacant in 1724, so that no report was made for it then, but the county records

---

[35]Perry, *Historical Collections*, I, p. 292.
[36]*William and Mary College Quarterly*, VI, p. 82.
[37]Fothergill, *A List of Emigrant Ministers to America*, p. 24.
[38]There was also a St. Stephen's Parish in King and Queen County.

show that in 1702 John Farnefold, the minister of the parish, who died in that year, left a part of his property for the establishment and maintenance of a school for poor children belonging to the parish. The section of the will which indicates his intention is as follows:

I give 100 acres where I now live for the maintenance of a free school to be called Winchester schoole for fower or five poore children belonging to ye parish and to be taught gratis & to have their dyett lodging & washing & when they can read the Bible & write a legible hand to dismiss them & take in more, such as my exors., shall think fitt, and for the benefitt of the said school I give five cows and a Bull, six ewes, and a ram, a carthorse & cart and two breeding sowes, & that my two mulatto girles Frances and Lucy Murrey have a yeare's schooling & be free when they arrive at the age of 22 years to whom I give a sow shote to each, & for further encouragement of a schoolmaster, I give dyett, lodging & washing and 500 pds of tobacco & a horse, Bridle & Saddle to ride on during his stay, the place where the school house is to be erected my will is to have it neare my dwelling house, some part of which may serve for a school house till another more conveniently be built. Item what schoole books I have in my study I leave for ye benefit of ye schoole. Then my will is that some of my estate be sold for the maintenance of the said schoole except what my exors., shall think fitt to select necessary for use as bedding, potts, & pewter. . . .If the school fail for want of maintenance which I hope it will not give that hundred acres & all the rest of my land to Farnefold Nutt.[39]

It was clearly Farnefold's purpose to establish a boarding school, but it does not seem that he made sufficient provision for the operation of such an establishment for any length of time. The only evidence with regard to the school outside of the will is in a land patent to Farnefold Nutt which records that "John Farnefold, clerk, by his last will gave one hundred acres of land for ye use of a Free School.[40] The school was probably in operation for some years, but the small size of the foundation gift and the lack of reference to it in documents of a later period may mean that it was discontinued "for want of maintenance" which Farnefold had foreseen as a possibility. The alternative gift of the property to Nutt in case of its failure suggests that his interest may have interfered with the continued operation of the school.

There was one other bequest made before 1724 with the intent of founding a free parish school, but the evidence indicates that the purpose of the donor was not carried out. In 1685 William Gordon left one hundred acres of land to Christ Church Parish in Middlesex

---

[39]*William and Mary College Quarterly*, XVII, pp. 245–46. Farnefold seems to have named his school after Winchester Grammar School, which suggests that at one time he may have been a student there. He was a member of the first board of trustees of William and Mary College.
[40]*Virginia Magazine of History*, IV, p. 31.

County to establish a free school.[41]   The vestry record of the parish, which begins with the year 1670, contains no reference to the gift before 1727, in which year it was ordered by the vestry,

That the church wardens procure copies of the will of Mr. William Gordon relating to Land given to this parish for a free school.[42]

There is no further record in the vestry book relating to the Gordon bequest until 1748, at which time the parish began to receive annually 500 pounds of tobacco which was "employed towards the schooling of poor children."[43]   The income from the land was clearly insufficient to establish and maintain a free school, but the fact that the vestrymen did not take action regarding the grant until 1727 suggests that they lacked interest in the education of the poor.[44]

Besides the gifts to parishes made before 1724 for the foundation of free schools there was one bequest made for the purpose of aiding in the support of a parish school.   In 1668 Henry King, a resident of Upper Parish, Nansemond County, bequeathed one hundred acres of land to the parish "towards the maintenance of a free school."[45] The existing vestry book of Upper Parish covers only the period after 1744, but in this period there is no reference to the King bequest. The minister of the parish in 1724 reported that there was then "no public school" in it[46] and no evidence has been found to show that

---

[41]*William and Mary College, Quarterly*, VI, p. 82.
[42]MS. vestry record for October 10, 1727.
[43]*Ibid.*, record for years 1748 to 1767.
[44]Bruce (*Institutional History of Virginia*, I, 358) says with reference to the Gordon bequest,
    "William Gordon, of Middlesex, presented one hundred acres of valuable land as an endowment for a free school; and with the proceeds obtained from the sale of crops of this plantation, a schoolhouse was soon erected, and a regular teacher employed, who, for some years, gave instruction, without expense, to the children in attendance."
    The reference given as source for the statement quoted is an article by Tyler, *William and Mary College Quarterly*, VI, 82.   The statement in the *Quarterly* is as follows:
    In Middlesex, in 1685, William Gordon gave one hundred acres of land for a free school, on which land a schoolhouse was built; and school was conducted for some years.   In 1700 the court of Middlesex reported that the said school land "now lyeth idle."
    Tyler does not indicate the source of his information, but presumably the year of the bequest is given in the court record of wills.   The data taken from the vestry record and given above make it seem improbable that the school was actually established.
[45]The part of the will relating to the gift is as follows:
    I give one hundred Acres of land lieing & beinge Adjacent to Mr. England and being exchanged for land of myne now in the possession of Mr. England to this parrish where I now live towards the maintenance of a free school.   (Will printed in *William and Mary College Quarterly*, V, p. 112).
[46]Perry, *Historical Documents*, I, p. 296.

there was one later. Probably the lack of a school to which the income from the King land could be given and the relative smallness of the gift explain the inaction of the vestrymen who were the officers responsible for the administration of the property. In 1754 the parish built a workhouse in which a number of children were cared for and taught, and it may be that the income from the King gift was placed in the parish funds without record and used for the support of this undertaking.

The data which have been presented above show that there were in Virginia in 1724 five endowed parish schools and that these probably constituted all but one of the endowed free schools in the colony at the time. The chief sources yielding information concerning the schools before 1724 are first the county, parish and colonial records, and second, the reports of the ministers in the colony to the Bishop of London. It is a significant fact that the number of endowed schools reported by the ministers corresponds closely with the number shown by other sources to have been in existence. If it had been found that there were several endowed schools which were not reported in 1724, either within the limits of the parishes reported upon or outside of them, it might be assumed that further investigation would reveal the existence of others. As has been stated, the county records have not been studied systematically enough to make it certain that all school facts they contain have been gleaned, but the correspondence between the survey report of 1724 and what the study of the county records already made has revealed makes it seem likely that the examination of them by various students has been fairly exhaustive. This applies to the period after 1724 as well as that before, and if this view is correct it justifies the drawing of conclusions regarding schools in the later period on the basis of what has already been found in the county records and published and what is revealed by the other available sources.

The parish schools founded before 1724 were the Syms, Eaton, Peasley, Sandford, and Horton schools. It was the custom for the founders of the free schools to place their management in the hands of parish or parish and county officials, making them in a sense public schools. The Syms School and the Eaton School were both in Elizabeth City Parish, so that only four of the twenty-nine parishes reported upon by the ministers in 1724 had endowed schools. In view of the fact that among the twenty-nine older and more thickly populated parishes only four had such institutions, it is not strange that in the twenty-six not reported upon the record of only one has been found.

ENDOWED PARISH SCHOOLS ESTABLISHED AFTER 1724

In the period after 1724 there were four endowed parish schools added to those in existence before that year. One of these was the second Peasley School to which reference has been made.

Bruton Parish in James County

In 1742 Mrs. Mary Whaley left to the care of the minister and church wardens of Bruton Parish, as representatives of the parish, a charity school known as Mattey's School, which she had established some years previously in memory of her son Matthew. The following extract from her will shows the nature of the gift and the character of the school:

I give devise and bequeath to the minister and churchwardens for the time being of the said parish of Bruton in the county of York in the said Colony of Virginia and their successors a certain piece of land in the said parish of Bruton containing by estimation ten acres little more or less together with Mattey's schoolhouse and a Dwelling house lately erected and built thereon for the use of a schoolmaster (to teach the neediest children of the Same parish who shall be offered in the art of reading writing and arithmetic). . . . .

I give to Mattey's School aforesaid the sum of Fifty pounds sterling to be paid to the said minister and churchwardens for the time being and their successors at the rate of ten pounds a year for the use of the same school.[47]

The money grant to the school was not made available during the colonial period,[48] but the trustees apparently had no difficulty in getting a master to teach a number of poor children in return for the use of the property and the right which was probably given him of taking in pay pupils. In 1750 the trustees stated that the "school and the Teaching therein hath continued" without interruption after the death of Mrs. Whaley in 1742.[49] In 1766 they placed the following advertisement in the *Williamsburg Gazette:*

Mattey Free School, Williamsburg, Sep. 4, 1766.
The trustees for Mrs. Whaley's charity to Mattey's School (the minister and churchwardens of Bruton Parish) give this notice, that in the forenoone of Monday they will meet in the church of Williamsburg to choose a Master for that school.

---

[47]*William and Mary College Quarterly,* IV, pp. 10, 13. The Whaley will as well as other source material bearing on the history of the Mattey School has been published by Lyon G. Tyler in the *Quarterly.*
[48]*Ibid.,* VI, p. 79.
[49]*Ibid.,* IV, p. 7.

They hope to have it in their power to make such proposals as shall encourage a diligent and useful person to accept of the office.[50]

In 1768 the *Gazette* announced that Mr. William Rose had succeeded the late Mr. Jacob Bruce as master.[51] While the Mattey School did not have as great an endowment as some of the other parish schools, its location in Williamsburg favored it, and it probably was in successful operation from 1742 until the end of the colonial period, at any rate.[52]

Suffolk Parish in Nansemond County

Some time before 1731 John Yeates of Suffolk Parish in Nansemond County established two schools for the education of the children in the neighborhood in which he lived. In his will, drawn up in 1731, he provided by endowment for the support of the schools and arranged that the members of the parish vestry resident in the part of the parish near his home should manage them.[53] Nothing concerning the conduct of the schools after 1731 has been found, but the income from the bequest was apparently sufficient to carry out Yeates' intentions, for in 1804 after the property had been converted it consisted in nineteen slaves who were hired out for forty-eight pounds annually.[54]

[50] *William and Mary College Quarterly*, IV, p. 10.
[51] *Ibid.*, XXVII, p. 209.
[52] The vestry book of Bruton Parish is lost or destroyed, and the extracts from it which were published in 1855 in *The Church Review and Ecclesiastical Record* contain no reference to the Mattey School.
[53] Yeates' will is given in the *Virginia School Report for 1885*, Third Part, pp. 230–31. The sections relating to the schools are as follows:
"I give and bequeath all my land or lands in Virginia, and all the rents and profits of the same to the following use and uses: The rents thereof, now by lease or otherwise, may be converted hereafter to the use of a free-school or schools, in the lower part of Nansemond, formerly so called, being the parish I have so long lived in, among such friendly neighbors; and that there may be two school-houses continued in the same places already fixed, which I have built, so that one schoolhouse will be very convenient for the children of the one side of Bennett's Creek, and the other on the other side thereof, which will complete that part of the parish, as formerly I have done; and by that means, with God's blessing, the most or all of the children in those parts will be educated from the Glebe down to the extent of that part of the parish lying on the south side of Nansemond river, which formerly was called the Lower Parish of Nansemond."
"What books I have or shall give for the use of the school or schools, may lie in the desk in the schoolhouse, under lock and key, in each schoolhouse as I have provided, that when children have read those books they may be there ready for other children also."
The will then provides for a gift of 10£, "to buy books for the poorer sort of inhabitants in the parish, as the Whole Duty of Man; also for procuring Testaments, Psalters, Primers, for my several schools."
The provision regarding the management of the property is as follows:
"It is my will and desire that those gentlemen vestrymen living this side of Nansemond river may have the management of the disposal of the rent yearly."
[54] *Ibid.*, p. 230.

Besides the Yeates schools and the Mattey School there were a number of endowed schools founded in the latter part of the colonial period, but none of them seems to have been given to a parish or placed in charge of parish officials.[55] There were, however, several gifts of property to parishes for the purpose of providing free education for poor children in private schools or of assisting in such provision. The largest grant for the support of education of the poor of which record has been found is that of Humphrey Hill of the Parish of St. Stephen's in King and Queen County. In 1775 Hill gave 500 pounds to the minister, wardens, and vestrymen of the parish,

to be by them put out at interest on land security, and the interest becoming due or arising thereon to be annually paid to such schoolmasters as shall teach one or more children whose parents are unable to pay for the instruction of such child or children themselves.[56]

NUMBER, MANAGEMENT, AND CHARACTER OF PARISH SCHOOLS, 1634-1775

The data which have been presented show that there were in colonial Virginia nine endowed parish schools six of which were entirely in the control of parish officials, the others being in charge of boards of trustees made up of both parish and county officers. Since only seven of the ninety parishes existing at the end of the colonial period had endowed schools, it is clear that we should look upon them as being exceptional rather than common arrangements for educating parish children. The work of parish endowed schools was to an extent supplemented by several free schools for poor children which were not in control of public officials but these were fewer in number and of less consequence than the others. The distinction between the parish endowed schools and the similar institutions not under parish control is of course of little significance except for the fact that we are here concerned with public activity with the idea of

---

[55]In 1760, or thereabouts, William Hunter editor of the *Williambsurg Gazette*, bequeathed property for the support of a negro school in Williamsburg. For a time this school admitted white children as well as negroes. This fact is brought out in a letter of Rev. C. Nicholas to Rev. John Waring, who was an official of the S. P. G. in London. Nicholas states that,

"Soon after Mr. Hunter's Death I had the number of children increased to 30 & obliged the mistress that there might be no partiality shewn to white scholars, of which she then had about a dozen, to discharge them all & this at the Risque of the Displeasure of their Parents, with whom she was in high Repute for her Care & Method of Teaching" (*S. P. G. Minute Book* C, p. 69).

Mrs. Elizabeth Stith in 1774 left a bequest of 120 pounds to endow scholarships for six poor children in a school in Smithfield in Isle of Wight County which she had established in 1753 (*William and Mary College Quarterly*, V, 113).

[56]*William and Mary College Quarterly*, XVII, p. 247.

determining its extent and character and of finding the elements in it which might serve as a basis for later public education.[57]

It seems clear that the endowed parish schools as a whole were not considered very seriously or managed very carefully by those to whose care they were entrusted. The Eaton School was probably the most important of the free schools, but as has been shown above, its trustees for a long period neglected properly to make use of and guard its property or supervise the conduct of the school. The evidence indicates that the same is true of the Syms and Peasley schools. In the case of the other schools there is no basis for a judgment with regard to their management. The attitude of those in control of the schools may have been partially a reflection of the difficult conditions under which the institutions operated, making full success inherently impossible. No doubt the wide distribution of the population interfered with attendance, and probably the poor did not show much of a desire to make use of their educational opportunities. The large size of the parishes made it impossible for a school to serve more than a small district in its immediate neighborhood so that it could not be looked upon as a community enterprise of concern to the parish as a whole. But if the controlling class to which the parish school trustees belonged had had a keen interest in the education of the poor or had appreciated fully their responsibility, they would have exercised a closer supervision of their trust and would have shown their concern in a variety of ways which would have been evidenced in the records. At no time did the parish or colonial authorities attempt to supplement the income of the schools so that their work might be improved or extended. From the standpoint of later development of public activity in education the evidence of a desire on the part of the trustees to make the most of the free schools would have been more significant than the particular degree of success attained in their operation.

With the possible exception of the Eaton School the endowed parish schools in colonial Virginia were of the elementary vernacular type rather than Latin schools or institutions combining instruction in English and Latin. That is, they were essentially like the endowed non-classical schools of England to which reference has been made.

[57]Cubberley (*Public Education in the United States*, p. 22) states that in colonial Virginia there were "church charity schools for some of the children of the poorer members." The parish free endowed schools were the nearest approach to institutions of the type mentioned by him, for in no case did the Established Church in Virginia provide a school.

That this was the fact is shown directly in the cases of the Horton, Farnefold, Mattey, and Yeates schools. The only evidence suggesting that Latin was taught in any of the schools is in the use of the term "free school" in application to them and in the requirement of the master of the Eaton School in 1697 that he should instruct in "gramer learninge."

The application of the term "free school" to the endowed establishments of the type considered is sometimes taken to mean that they gave Latin instruction,[58] and there is a slight basis in colonial usage for this interpretation.[59] A Virginia statute of 1656 provided for the apprenticing of orphan boys where the estates "will not reach to a free education,"[60] thereby implying that there was a distinction between the English instruction which a master was required by law to give his apprentice and a "free education" suitable for boys in families of property. In England this education consisted mainly in Latin instruction and it was commonly given in Latin grammar schools to which the term "free school" was often applied. In 1660-61 the General Assembly provided for the purchase of land for a "colledge and freeschoole,"[61] although the project was not then carried out. In 1690 Governor Nicholson proposed the revival of the "design of a free school and colledge." The interest of those who were back of the plan was evidently not in establishing a school where education free from cost could be given; it was rather in providing an

---

[58]In referring to the free schools in Virginia in the seventeenth century, Bruce (*Institutional History of Virginia*, I, p. 350) speaks of their models as being the endowed grammar schools of England and says, "There was not a single shire in England lacking one of these fine grammar schools." While it is likely that if conditions in Virginia had been more favorable free grammar schools would have been established there, it is clear that the models for the schools actually established were the non-classical schools of England rather than the Latin schools.

[59]In reference to the use of "free school" in connection with English grammar schools in the 16th and 17th centuries, Leach (*English Schools at the Reformation*, p. 110) says, "What was the meaning of Free School, or Free Grammar School at this time? Dr. Johnson defined it to mean, and that is the obvious meaning of it, a school that is free,—where no payment is made for tuition fees." Jackson (*School Support in Colonial Massachusetts*, p. 86) says with respect to the meaning of the term "free school" as used in Massachusetts, "On the basis of the records themselves we may assert that the primary meaning of the term 'free school' as used in Massachusetts meant freedom from charges for being taught." However, this statement is not opposed to the view that the term was occasionally used to indicate a Latin school. In 1753 there were in Boston two free writing schools and one free Latin school. In the town records for that year a committee reported that they had "also obtained Copys of the Grant, Survey, and Return of one Thousand Acres of Land for the Free School of Boston." (*Boston Town Records, 1729-1742*, p. 110). This is in evident reference to the Latin school.

[60]Hening, Statutes, I, p. 416.

[61]Hening, II, 25. A similar use of the term occurs in a Maryland law of 1663 (Clews, p. 408).

opportunity for students to prepare themselves to meet the college entrance requirements.

If there were many other illustrations in Virginia colonial records of the use of "free" with an implication like that indicated above, there might be a presumption in the case of any free school that it gave instruction in Latin unless there is positive evidence to the contrary. In fact the instances mentioned are the only ones found in the course of the present study.[62] The typical use of "free school" as meaning a school free from tuition for those for whom it was founded is shown in Farnefold's will given above. Property was given to found,

a free school . . . for fower or five poore children . . . to be taught gratis . . . & when they can read the Bible & write a legible hand to dismiss them.

The only parishes reported in 1724 as having within their limits a Latin school were Bruton and Elizabeth City. The Bruton Parish school was the "Grammar School" connected with the College, while the school in Elizabeth City Parish was a "private school." The emphasis which the minister of Elizabeth City Parish put upon the fact that Latin and Greek, in addition to reading, writing, and ciphering, were taught in the private school without mentioning them as subjects taught in the Syms School or the Eaton School tends to show that neither of the endowed schools at the time regularly gave Latin instruction. None of the general treatises on conditions and customs in Virginia mentions Latin as a subject taught in any of the free schools. In Hugh Jones' *Present State of Virginia*, published in 1724, there is a proposed plan of education for the colony. Jones speaks of the existence of reading and writing schools in the parishes, and then says,

Let such lads as have been taught to read and write in those schools, be admitted into the Grammar School at the College.[63]

---

[62]It may have been that Governor Berkeley in his well-known statement concerning education in Virginia in 1671 used "free schools" in its exceptional meaning. He said, "But I thank God, there are no free schools nor printing, and I hope we shall not have these hundred years; for learning has brought disobedience and heresy, and sects into the world, and printing has divulged them" (Hening, II, 37). If we should understand that Berkeley was referring to Latin schools, which is quite possible, his statement should be accepted as evidence that Latin was not taught in the Eaton or Syms free schools which were then in operation. This interpretation makes it unnecessary to conclude that his statement was false. There is a suggestion that this interpretation may be correct in the fact that in the apprentice law of 1656 and the enactment of 1660–61 providing land "for a colledge and freeschoole," which were passed in his administration, "free" is used to indicate Latin school instruction—as has been shown above.

[63]*Present State of Virginia*, p. 84.

If the several free schools of the time were giving Latin instruction, he probably would have recognized the fact in his scheme.

The requirement that the master of the Eaton School in 1697 should instruct in "gramer learninge" as well as in English must be taken to mean that at the time Latin grammar was taught in the school. It seems likely that for a time following and preceding 1697 the subject was taught, for the conditions under which the school operated did not change. That Latin was not taught regularly in the school or that it was a minor interest is shown by what has been brought out above. Eaton did not say in his will what subjects were to be taught, but that his use of "free school" was the customary one is indicated by his statement that in it "no free education" should be given except to those for whom it was founded.

Except in the case of the Eaton School, wherever there is any direct evidence regarding subjects taught in the free parish schools it shows that they were the branches commonly taught in the vernacular schools of the time—reading and writing, or reading, writing, and arithmetic—and we may assume that these subjects were taught in all of them.[64] The requirement that the master of the Eaton School should instruct "all such children in English" as came to him merely meant that he should give instruction in the subjects commonly taught in the vernacular. Although religion was not definitely prescribed as a subject of instruction as were reading, writing, and arithmetic, it is probable that the teachers followed the universal custom of the time, catechizing children and using religious material in reading. Farnefold provided in his will that the children who should be in attendance at his school at any time were to be replaced by others as soon as they could "read the Bible and write a legible hand." In the will of John Yeates to which reference has been made there is provision for a gift for procuring "Testaments, Psalters, Primers, for my several schools." The minister reporting for Henrico Parish in 1724 said that children in private schools were catechized by their teachers,[65] and if this was the case in the private schools it was no doubt the practice in the free schools. Some of the apprenticeship laws required masters to instruct in the Christian

[64]Graves, in his *History of Education in Modern Times*, p. 85, states that the free schools increased in number in the 18th century "and their courses were much improved." There is no evidence in the case of any of the schools showing a change or improvement in the course of study.

[65]Perry, *Historical Documents*, I, p. 305.

religion the children bound to them,[66] and in accordance with this provision the indentures often stipulated that apprentices should be taught so far as to be able to read the Bible.

It was evidently the primary purpose of the founders of the endowed schools in Virginia to provide education for the poor. In the cases of the Farnefold, Sandford, and Mattey schools this is specifically stated as the intention. Eaton spoke in his will of the education of "children," but that this was understood to mean poor children is indicated in the Act of 1759 incorporating the trustees of the Eaton School where they are referred to as "the proper objects of the pious founder's charity." Yeates seems to have been the only founder who had in mind provision for all the children of a district. In providing educational facilities for the poor the men who endowed the schools seem to have been moved less by religious interest than were those who established the English schools for the poor or the public schools in New England.[67] They did not indicate in their wills that they had pious intentions nor do they mention religious upbringing or instruction. While they no doubt assumed that the schools they founded would teach religion, according to the custom of the time, their concern apparently was primarily in giving the poor an opportunity to better themselves. Probably the lack of religious motives back of the settlement of Virginia and the general conformity among the people to the beliefs of the Established Church made religious instruction in schools seem less important than in most of the other colonies. The point of significance here is that the lack of

---

[66]Hening, I, 260–61.

[67]The following are typical statements showing the emphasis on religion in English charity education in the seventeenth and eighteenth centuries. In Basingstoke in 1618 James Deane left 13 £ to be devoted to the payment of a petty schoolmaster, "who shall teach little children to write and read but especially to read and to learn the catechism in the principles of religion" (quoted by Watson, *English Grammar Schools*, p. 153). In *An Account of Charity Schools Lately Erected*, published in 1709, it is stated that the chief design of the schools "is for the Education of Poor Children in the Rules and Principles of the Christian Religion as professed and taught in the Church of England. . . ." The importance attached to religious education in the Puritan colonies is suggested by the following extract from the Connecticut code of 1656: Parents and masters must educate the children in their charge so that they "may, through God's blessing, attain at least so much as to be able duly to read the Scriptures and other good and profitable printed books in the English tongue, being their native language, and in some competent measure to understand the main grounds and principles of Christian religion necessary to salvation, and to give a due answer to such plain and ordinary questions as . . . may be propounded concerning the same" (Clews, *Colonial Educational Legislation*, p. 79). No such statements as the above are found in the sources dealing with education in colonial Virginia.

a strong religious purpose kept down the number of endowed institutions and lessened in a measure the interest of those in whose charge the schools were left.

Although it was the object of the founders of the parish free schools to provide education for the poor, it is evident that children in better class families as well as those whose parents could not afford to pay for their tuition commonly received instruction in them. Probably it was ordinarily expected that parents who were able to pay tuition should do so, for in most cases the income from the foundation grant was small. Beverley, writing in 1705, spoke of the "allowance" paid the masters of the endowed schools by "gentlemen" whose sons attended them.[68] The perquisites referred to in the advertisement appearing in the *Williamsburg Gazette* in 1753, which the master of the Syms School received in addition to the income from the school farm, very probably were in the form of fees paid by some of the pupils. The income from the Mattey School was clearly insufficient to support a master. We have seen that for some time previous to 1759 children of parents "well able to pay for their education" had attended the Eaton School without charge, but that the abuse was then corrected.[69]

In specifying who should be instructed in the endowed parish schools the founders speak of "children" without indicating whether they intended that girls should attend. While it is likely that girls in colonial Virginia received schooling less commonly than boys, in accordance with the general custom of the time, there is sufficient evidence to show that many in both the upper and lower classes were given an education. The common provision in indentures binding girls to apprenticeship, that they should be taught to read, shows an attitude favorable to their education. These facts taken in connection with the lack of any suggestion of discrimination against them makes it seem probable that they attended the public parish schools.[70]

[68] Beverley, *History of Virginia*, p. 40.

[69] Cubberley (*Public Education in the United States*, p. 21) speaks of Virginia as illustrating the "non-state interference, pauper-school attitude," apparently meaning that the endowed free schools were pauper schools. The attendance of children from the better class shows that the schools were not looked down upon. The situation of the children who were admitted without charge was not unlike that of foundationers in the endowed English grammar schools.

[70] The only suggestion that girls may not have attended the endowed schools which has been found in the course of the present study is in a statement in Beverley's *History* having to do with the situation in 1705. In reference to support of the schools Beverley said that besides incomes from foundation grants the masters received "an additional allowance which gentlemen give with their

There is no statement in the sources showing exactly how many pupils there were at any time in any of the endowed parish schools. It is probable that the children of appropriate age who lived sufficiently near a school attended it, but their number must have been relatively small. According to the ministers who reported in 1724 there was on the average one family per square mile in the parishes having endowed schools,[71] and Elizabeth City, relatively the most thickly populated parish, had only slightly more than this. All of the parish institutions which have been mentioned were located on the plantations which the founders gave for their support except the Mattey School and possibly the Yeates schools. None of the founders, with the above exceptions, seems to have questioned the suitability of his farm from the standpoint of nearness to the homes of children whose parents might wish them to attend, but this is presumably a reflection of the fact that there was little concentration of population to be taken into account. If the situation had been otherwise each donor probably would have provided for the sale or lease of his property and the establishment of a school in a section where homes were relatively close together.

In the case of the Peasley School we have direct evidence showing that the distance from homes interfered with attendance. The school was established in the seventeenth century, but until 1756, when the trustees were incorporated, there were so "few children" frequenting it because of its "inconvenient situation" that it had been of little benefit. Farnefold made detailed provision in his will for a free school in which "fower or five poore children" were to be educated and maintained. It seems likely that his reason for not suggesting that day pupils living near his plantation might attend and thus provide sufficient work for the master and enlarge the service of the school was that he thought the school would not be near enough to the homes of the children to allow them to attend. An indication of the influence of the plantation system in interfering with efforts to instruct children in groups is given in the statement of the minister in South Farnham Parish in 1724 with reference to his practice in catechizing on Sunday.[72] He stated that

sons" implying that the daughters in the upper class families at least did not attend. The only direct reference in the wills of founders of endowed schools to the instruction of girls is in Farnefold's will, quoted above, where provision is made for a year's schooling of two mulatto girls. This suggests that white girls were not discriminated against.

[71]Perry, *Historical Documents*, I, pp. 262–318.
[72]*Ibid.*, I, p. 286.

"the remoteness of the parishioners from church prevents their sending their children to be catechized." South Farnham at the time was one of the relatively more densely populated parishes.[73]

The Eaton School apparently had a larger number of pupils than any other similar institution. Reference has been made to the assertion in the Act of 1759 incorporating its trustees that,

the said foundation hath been abused by admitting a great number of children into the said school, whose parents are well able to pay for their education.

The statement does not mean that at any one time there had been a great number of children of the well-to-do in the school; it means, rather, that the total number of better class children who had attended over a period of years was large, and that their free education constituted an abuse. However, it is probable that nothing would have been done to limit or prohibit their attendance if a fairly large number had not sought instruction in it. The relatively good attendance in the Eaton School may be accounted for partially by the fact that Elizabeth City Parish in which it was situated had a

---

[73]The following extract from *The Present State of Virginia*, written in 1697 by Hartwell, Chilton, and Blair, is an aid in visualizing the condition of affairs at the middle of the colonial period. The system of industry which brought about the condition described continued throughout the colonial period.

"As to the outward Appearance, it looks all like a wild Desert; the Highlands overgrown with Trees, and the Lowlands sunk with Water, Marsh, and Swamp: The few Plantations and clear'd Grounds bearing no proportion to the rough and uncultivated . . . perhaps not the hundredth Part of the Country is yet clear'd from the Woods, and not one Foot of the Marsh and Swamp drained, as fast as the Ground is worn out with Tobacco and Corn, it runs up again in underwoods, and in many Places of the Country, that which has been cleared is thicker in Woods than it was before the clearing. It is but in few Places that the Plough is made use of, for in their first clearing they never grub up the Stumps, but cut the Trees down about two or three Foot from the Ground; so that all the Roots and Stumps being left, that Ground must be tended with Hoes, and by that time the Stumps are rotten the Ground is worn out; and having fresh Land enough, of which they must clear some for Firewood, they take but little care to recruit the old Fields". . . (pp. 6 and 7).

The relation between education and the conditions suggested above is pointed out by various contemporary writers. The following is from a statement made in 1705.

"Cohabitation would highly advance Learning and school education: for this flourishes only in such places, for the smallest and meanest of Schools cannot be maintained without a competent number of Scholars, which has been our great discouragement in *Virginia* and *Maryland* where the number to be entertained together are too few to maintain any master or mistress, who are necessitated to shift from place to place, until they cannot live at all by that Calling: so that in many remote corners many families never had opportunities of schools, and therefore remain without all knowledge of Letters, which we have no hopes of regulating or preventing without Towns and Cohabitation" (Francis Makemie, "A Plain and Friendly Perswasive to the Inhabitants of Virginia and Maryland, 1705", *Va. Mag. of Hist. and Biog.*, IV, p. 255).

population less widely distributed than any other which had an endowed school excepting Bruton Parish. The school also seems to have been the best of the endowed institutions, as is suggested by the fact that Latin was taught in it at least for a time.

CHAPTER IV

EDUCATION IN THE PARISH WORKHOUSE

The English workhouses of the seventeenth and eighteenth centuries, with which the Virginia colonists were familiar, were often educational institutions as well as establishments for the care and employment of the poor. The common idea among the many variations in these houses of industry was that the inmates, whether children or adults, should aid in their support as far as possible by engaging in various occupations, usually in converting textiles, and in order to make the plan of production effective it was often necessary to give a small amount of trade instruction.[1] In the seventeenth century, particularly before the Civil War, when the workhouses were at their best as industrial establishments,[2] intensive trade education was also given to youths of apprentice age in some of the institutions then in operation, with the purpose of developing skilled workers who could later maintain themselves and contribute to the industrial good of the country.[3]

One of the best industrial schools within a workhouse was that of the London Bridewell as conducted in the first half of the seventeenth century, in which training in numerous occupations was given to the youths confined there at the hands of arts masters to whom they were apprenticed.[4] "Christ's Hospital at Ipswich, the Hospital at Reading,

---

[1]Leonard, *English Poor Relief*, pp. 225–27; Dunlop, *English Apprenticeship*, p. 248; Gray, *A History of English Philanthropy*, p. 114.

[2]Gray, pp. 216, 220; Leonard, p. 238.

[3]Leonard, p. 217.

[4]In a report of the London Bridewell made in 1630–31, quoted by Leonard, p. 354, there is the following statement concerning the number of apprentices and their trades:

"Four Silkeweavers who doe keepe poore children taken vp in the streets or otherwise distressed as their apprentices to the number of fortye & sixe.

Two Pinmakers who doe likewise keepe as apprentices twenty and three.

One Ribbon weaver who keepeth v apprentices.

Two Hempdressers who keepe Tenn apprentices.

Five Glovers who keepe Sixteene apprentices.

One Linnen Weav (er) who keepeth iii jr apprentices.

and the Nottingham House of Correction had all training departments of this kind in which many of the poor children of these towns were taught trades."[5]

The inmates of the English workhouses of the eighteenth century were chiefly decrepit old people and children too young to be apprenticed.[6] In order that the children might take part in the simple industrial activities carried on, and thus contribute to their support and "be inured betimes to labor," they were given a small amount of training in such occupations as carding, spinning, knitting, and stocking making. At various ages from eight to twelve they were commonly bound out as apprentices so that the public might be relieved entirely from the costs of their maintenance. Instruction other than that of a manual type was seldom given in the seventeenth century workhouses, but in the eighteenth century the children were usually taught to read and say the catechism, and less often, to write and "cast accompts." This instruction was given in some of the institutions when the children were very young before they were set to work, in others at the age when they were working. The school within the workhouse was in some cases supported out of the rates, in others by charitable gifts.[7]

One Carpenter who keepeth Two apprentices.
The whole number of apprentices are cvi."
Manchester in 1615 made an arrangement with John Kirby whereby he agreed to "diligently teach, instructe and bringe upp all such youthes, children and other persons as shall be sent or committed into the said Howse of Correcon in some honest and true labour soe longe as they shall remayne there vnder his chardge" (Quoted by Leonard, p. 228).

[5]Leonard, *English Poor Relief*, p. 218.
[6]Gray, *History of English Philanthropy*, p. 115.
[7]An Account of Several Workhouses (London, 1732). This gives a detailed account of the operation of more than one hundred parish workhouses. Following is the regulation regarding the education of the children in the workhouse of St. Giles Parish:
"That there be a school in the House, where all children above three Years of Age, shall be kept till they be five years old, and then set to spinning, knitting, or to such other work as shall be thought proper for the Benefit of the Parish, and that the Master or Mistress who shall teach them to Work, or some other proper Person, shall likewise instruct each of them in Reading twice a Day, half an Hour each time, till they are nine years of Age; and then that the said Master or Mistress, or other proper Person, do teach them to write and cast Accompts two hours every Day, the better to qualify them for Apprenticeship or Services"(p. 31).
In the Parish of Stepney,
"The Children in this House are all young and helpless, and therefore are sent to a School in the neighborhood, at the publick charge, till they are 8 years of Age; and then they are bound out apprentices till the Age of 24" (p. 68).
In a parish workhouse in Northamptonshire the working school was so successfully conducted by a man and his wife that there were forty children besides sixty parish children in it (p. 151).

The system of workhouses established by parishes in England had its beginning in local acts,[8] but in 1722 Parliament passed a general law giving to all parishes, singly or in union, permission to establish them.[9] As a result a large number of institutions were organized, as many as one hundred parishes being reported in 1725 as having taken advantage of it in the three years succeeding its passage.[10]

PARISH WORKHOUSE SCHOOLS IN VIRGINIA

The problem of caring for the poor in Virginia was relatively simple, and it was not until the latter part of the colonial period, when there was an increase in the number of the poor, that there was any attempt to provide workhouses as a means of lowering public charges and reducing the number of vagabonds. The indigent were well taken care of in the homes of the inhabitants or aided in their own homes, and dependent children were bound out at an early age as servants or apprentices, thus relieving the parish from costs for their maintenance. The possibility of using workhouses as a means of trade education, however, was recognized by the authorities, and in the seventeenth century two attempts were made by the General Assembly to establish them with this object in view. The intention seems to have been to set up institutions something like the training department of the Christ's Hospitals in England.

The first workhouse law, passed in 1646, provided in some detail for the establishment of a "flax house" at Jamestown to which children were to be sent from the different counties, there to be instructed and employed "in carding, knitting, and spinning, etc . . . under such master or mistresse as shall there be appointed."[11]   Only

---

[8]Webb, *English Local Government*, p. 130.

[9]George I, cap. 7. "IV . . . and for the greater ease of parishes in the relief of the poor, be it further enacted by the authority of the aforesaid, That it shall and may be lawful for the churchwardens and overseers of the poor in any parish, town, township or place, in vestry or other parish or publick meeting for that purpose assembled . . . to purchase or hire any house or houses in the same parish, township, or place, and to contract with any person or persons for the lodging, keeping, maintaining and imploying any or all such poor in their respective parishes, townships, or places."

[10]Nicholls, *History of the English Poor Law*, II, pp. 16–17.

[11]Hening, I, p. 336. The law provided,

"That the commissioners of the several counties respectively do, at their discretion, make choice of two children in each county of the age of eight or seven years at the least, either male or female, which are to be sent up to James City between this and June next. . .And that the said children be furnished from the said county with six barrels of corne, two coverlets, or one rugg and one blanket: One bed, one wooden bowl or tray, two pewter spoons, a sow shote of six months old, two laying hens, with convenient apparel both linen and woolen."

The law then goes on to indicate the dimensions of the houses to be built.

children of "such parents who by reason of their poverty are disabled to maintaine and educate them" were to be taken, but this provision was made probably because the authorities would not have been justified in forcibly taking others. There was no occasion at the time for establishing the institution as a means of caring for dependent children, since the system of apprenticeship readily effecte this end. The purpose was educational and industrial, and the law was merely one of a series enacted from 1633 to 1696 in a rather unsuccessful endeavor to further the cultivation of flax and the manufacture of linen.[12] As one evidence of the lack of success attending the efforts made, there is the statement of Governor Berkeley made in 1666 to the effect that he had incurred an expense of one thousand pounds in flax culture but had accomplished nothing by it.[13]

The statute of 1646 was repealed in 1661–62 without having been put into effect,[14] its failure being evidenced by the lack of success in raising flax up to the time of its repeal, the lack of further legislative regulations dealing with its execution, the provision of a new plan in 1668, and by the fact that no trace of it has been found in the records. We are not directly concerned with its operation, however, because it did not provide for any activity on the part of the parishes.

In 1668 a statute was enacted with the same general intent as that in the earlier law, but in this provision was made for the establishment of a number of county-parish institutions, wool and hemp in addition to flax are mentioned as commodities with which children were to work, and there was no requirement that action should be taken, the law merely giving permission.[15]

The detailed provision for the food and clothing of the children may be taken as evidence of the extreme care with which the project was planned, but it would have been more to the point to have effectively provided for the manufacture or importation of spinning wheels and the production of flax.

[12]Hening, I, p. 218; II, 26, 121, 306; III, p. 81.
[13]Bruce, *Economic History of Virginia*, I, p. 398.
[14]Hening, II p. 43.
[15]"An act impowering countie courts to build worke houses assisted by the vestrie
WHEREAS the prudence of all states ought as much as in them lyes to endeavor the propagation and encrease of all manufactures conducing to the necessityes of their subsistence, and God having blessed this country with a soyle capable of producing most things necessary for the use of men, if industriously improved, *It is enacted by the grand assembly* and the authority thereof, that for the better converting wool, flax, hempe, and other commodities into manufactures, and for the increase of artificers in the country, that the commissioners of each county court, with the assistance of the respective vestries of the parishes in their counties, shall be and hereby are empowered to build houses for the educating and instructing poore children in the knowledge of spinning, weaving, and other

Whether or not any meaning should be attached to the fact that wool is mentioned first in the list of commodities to be converted, it is certain that at the time of the passage of the law there was a special interest in the development of the woolen industry. In 1659 the exportation of wool was prohibited,[16] and in 1666 a law was passed requiring that "the commissioners of each county court shall provide and sett up a loom and weaver in each of the respective counties of this country, and at the charge of the county."[17] The interference of the Dutch with the trade connections with England in 1667 brought home to the Virginians the desirability of doing more than had been done in developing home manufacture of necessities such as woolen cloth.[18] The effort here was no more successful than in the case of linen. Beverley, writing in 1705, said, "Their sheep yield good Increase, and bear good Fleeces, but they shear them only to cool them."[19]

The Act of 1668 does not indicate what was to be the nature of the assistance to be given the courts by the vestries, but no doubt it was intended that they should have a part in the organization and conduct of the institutions as well as in their support. In case a work school was established in any community the vestry records should show something of the action taken by the vestry. The evidence of the joint meetings of the court and vestry might appear only in the court record, but the vestry book should indicate something of what was done by the parish officials in determining the policy to be pursued in co-operation with the court, and in particular it should show the action taken by the vestrymen or wardens in making choice of poor children to be cared for and educated in the institutions. Votes showing the levy of parish taxes for the support of the work-house also should appear. Only four of the vestry books extant begin as early as 1668, but neither in these or in those covering the later period is there any suggestion that the county-parish work-schools were actually founded, and the probability is that the permission given the courts and vestries was not taken advantage of. The fact that those who have examined the county records have

---

useful occupations and trades, and power granted to take poore children from indigent parents to place them to worke in those houses" (Hening, II, 266).

[16]Hening, II, 488.

[17]*Ibid.*, p. 238.

[18]Osgood, *American Colonies in the Seventeenth Century*, III, p. 256; Bruce, *Economic History of Virginia in the Seventeenth Century*, I, p. 385.

[19]Beverley, *History of Virginia*, p. 255.

reported nothing showing their organization further substantiates this conclusion.[20]

There was no further legislative attempt made in Virginia to set up workhouses for the purpose of trade education, but in 1755 an Act in general like the English law of 1722 was passed providing for them as a part of the scheme of poor relief. At the middle of the eighteenth century there was an increase in the number of poor people, particularly of the vagabond class, and it was with the purpose of furnishing a test of destitution and willingness to work, as well as of reducing the costs of poor support that the law was enacted. Following are the first two paragraphs of the law of 1755:

I. WHEREAS the number of poor people hath of late years much increased throughout this colony, and it will be the most proper method for their maintenance, and for the prevention of great mischiefs arising from such numbers of unemployed poor, to provide houses for their reception and employment,

II. BE it enacted . . . that it shall and may be lawful for the vestry of every parish in this colony to order and cause to be erected, purchased, or hired, one or more house or houses within their parish for the lodging, maintaininge, and employing of all such poor people as shall be upon the parish, or who shall desire relief from the vestry or church wardens; . . . and to levy a reasonable allowance in their parish levies, for the education of such poor children as shall be placed in the said house, or houses, until they shall be bound out according to law.[21]

Other paragraphs of the law provided that the poor should not move from one parish to another to gain a settlement, that beggars should be sent to the workhouse, and that a person who asked alms should go to the workhouse if required.[22]

[20]Bruce, in his *Economic History of Virginia*, I, p. 256, says in reference to the law of 1668, "This act must have been enforced, for in 1678 the justices of the peace of Lower Norfolk County were indicted by the Grand Jury for neglecting to observe it." (*Records of Lower Norfolk County*, original volume, 1675–1686, p. 40). He refers to the fact that Lord Culpeper as Governor received instructions in 1679 to further the erection of workhouses, and suggests that those established in response to the law of 1668 may have fallen into disuse. There must have been some exceptional circumstance obligating the county court of Lower Norfolk County, for the law, as shown in quotation above, was merely permissive, and the directions to Lord Culpeper may be properly considered as further evidence that nothing was done in effecting the intent of the law.

[21]Hening, VI, p. 475.

[22]The law of 1755 had its origin in a petition of the minister, wardens, and vestry of the Parish of Bruton in which there is reference to the increase in the number of vagabonds in the parish. The introductory paragraph of the law, given above, makes it appear that the conditions in Bruton Parish were general in the Colony. The prayer to the General Assembly set forth, "That the charge of providing for the Poor of the said Parish, hath always been burthensome to the Inhabitants thereof, and of late Years hath much increased, which they conceive is owing to the great number of idle Persons that resort to the City of Williamsburg (situate in the said Parish) in publick times, who lurk about the Town, and

The statute went beyond the English law of 1722 in definitely allowing parish levies for education, but, as has been shown, in practice the English parishes often provided out of the rates for the instruction of the poor children in their workhouses. The educational provision is of interest apart from its actual results for the reason that it represents the first legislative action taken by the colony allowing public taxation for education, and thus it may be considered the first step toward public activity in this field taken in Virginia.

Judging from the existing vestry books, the first action in response to the law of 1755 was taken by Bristol Parish in Prince George County. In the record for the November meeting of that year appears the order,

That the church wardens apply to the Vestrys of Martins Brandon and Bath parish to know if they will join with this parish towards building a workhouse, to keep the poor of the three parishes in, pursuant to an Act of the General Assembly.[2]

No report from the wardens appears in the record, but in the meeting of November, 1756, it was ordered,

That Theodorick Bland apply to the Vestry of Brandon Parish to join this parish in building a workhouse for the poor of each parish.[24]

In a December meeting of the same year it was,

Ordered that Stephen Dewey, Alexander Bolling, Theodorick Bland, William Eaton do meet the persons appointed by the vestries of Brandon and Bath Parishes to agree in settling the terms of the poore house.[25]

The joint committee met, and in the vestry meeting of February 23, 1757, the Bristol Parish members reported its conclusions. The report is of special interest, apart from the project it proposes, because it presents the only description of the educational condition of poor children in Virginia in the eighteenth century which has been found. The report is as follows.

It is the opinion of this Committee that a Convenient House ought to be Rented for Entertaining the poor of the said Parishes, if to be had, but if not, that then Land ought to be bought & Convenient Houses to be built for the joint use of the said Parishes in proportion to the Number of Tithables in each of the said Parishes. This Committee having taken under their most serious Con-

---

Parts adjacent, till they gain a Settlement, and then become a charge to the Parish." The parish officers then go on to ask permission to establish a workhouse in the parish. In response a bill was brought out which gave permission to all parishes as in the law finally enacted (*Journals of the House of Burgesses*, volume for 1752–1755, May 16, 1755, p. 260).

[23]Bristol Parish vestry book, p. 160.
[24]*Ibid.*, p. 164.
[25]*Ibid.*, p. 164.

sideration the unhappy and indeed miserable Circumstances of the many poor Orphans and other poor Children, Inhabitants of the said Parishes whose parents are utterly unable to give them any Education and being desirous to render the said House as Beneficial as possible & that such poor Children should be brought up in a Religious, Virtuous & Industrious Course of Life so as to become usefull members of the Community, Have Resolved earnestly to recommend it to their Respective Vestries that they should join in a Petition to the General Assembly to procure an Act to enable the said Parishes to erect a FREE SCHOOL for educating the poor Children of the said Parishes in Reading, Writing and Arithmetic at the joint Expence of the said Parishes, and Uniting the same to the said Poorhouse Under such Rules, Orders and Directions as shall be most just and proper for perfecting so usefull and Charitable a Work, And in Order to facilitate the obtaining such Act to propose that the said Vestries should unite in opening Subscriptions that the Rich and Opulent & all other well disposed people may have an opportunity of Contributing towards so pious a design out of that STORE which the FATHER of Bounties hath bestowed on them.[26]

In accordance with the proposal of the committee the four members from Bristol Parish were directed by the vestry,

to Petition the General Assembly in conjunction with the Vestrys of Martins Brandon and Bath Parishes to obtain such Act as aforesaid.

Neither the Journals of the House of Burgesses nor the Minutes of the Council record the reception of the proposed petition, and very possibly it was not presented for the reason that the other parish vestries did not favor the plan. The next reference to the project in the Bristol vestry minutes is in the record for 1774:

Ordered that the Revd Mr. Harrison the C. Wardens Rob't Bolling Docr Theok Bland, or any three of them, be appointed For the Parish of Bristol, to agree with the Vestry of Brandon Parish, in Order to Purchase a Place to Errect a Poor House for the use of Bristol and Brandon Parish's.[27]

This order taken in connection with the fact that there is no other reference to the workhouse shows that the plan was not carried out.

While the law of 1755 contemplated merely the education of the few little children who might be cared for in each of the workhouses before the time of their apprenticeship, probably at the age of six or seven, the intention in the joint committee's report apparently was to establish a kind of boarding school for improperly cared for children whether or not they were actually dependent. If the school was to serve the three parishes, the distribution of the population meant that the children would have to live in the institution, and this together with the provision for instruction in "Reading, Writing,

---

[26]Bristol Parish vestry book, pp. 165–66.
[27]*Ibid.*, p. 244.

and Arithmetic'' without a reference to apprenticeship implied that the children to be taught might be from six to ten years of age or possibly older. There may have been an intention to make the institution a kind of working school like that established in Talbot County, Maryland, a few years previously, and largely with money raised in Virginia.[28] There is no indication of it in the report, however. It is clear that the idea was to go beyond what was allowed by the provisions of the law of 1755 for otherwise no special Act of the Assembly would have been required. Consideration of the statement in the report regarding the lack of educational provisions for the poor will be taken up later.[29]

The references in the vestry books to the establishment or operation of workhouses in response to the law of 1755 are very few and brief, and they give no suggestion of educational activity except in the one case cited. In fact the institutions established seem to have been poorhouses without provision for employment such as intended by the law. The vestry records show that the following six parishes had workhouses or poorhouses at the dates indicated: Frederick Parish in Louisa County (1756), Petsworth Parish in Gloucester County (1760), Christ Church Parish in Lancaster County (1767), Augusta Parish in Augusta County (1767), Elizabeth City Parish in Elizabeth City County (1771), and Stratton Major Parish in King and Queen County (1772).

[28]Steiner, *History of Education in Maryland*, p.34; *William and Mary College Quarterly*, XII, p. 162.

[29]The exceptional character of the proposition stated in the report of the joint committee raises the question as to whether it was an expression of a growing community interest in the education of the poor. A possible explanation is found by relating what is recorded in the Bristol Parish vestry minutes to some of the circumstances connected with the passage of the law of 1755. The extracts from the vestry record which have been given suggest that Theodorick Bland, perhaps the leading man in the community at the time, may have been the person most interested in the establishment of the parish school and most responsible for the action taken. The Journal of the House of Burgesses records that after the receipt of the petition from Bruton Parish, above referred to as being the occasion for the passage of the law of 1755, "a Bill for employing and better maintaining the Poor. . . .was read the first Time, and ordered read the second Time." Four days later the bill was read the second time and given to a committee of which Mr. Bland, from Prince George County, was a member. This committee brought in an amendment which was accepted, although what the amendment was is not indicated. The fact that the main difference between the English statute of 1722 and the Virginia law of 1755 was in the educational provision suggests that the amendment may have been the insertion of the educational clause. Mr. Bland's membership on the committee of the Assembly and on the committee of the vestries which brought forward the educational project, together with the fact that Bristol Parish was the first one to respond to the Act of 1755, suggests that he may have been responsible for the proposal as it appears in the Bristol vestry minutes.

While none of the parishes took advantage of the educational provisions of the law of 1755, there was one which established a poorhouse upon the basis of a grant of property left by will after obtaining a special Act of the Assembly, and upon its own initiative provided for the teaching of poor children within it. In a will made in 1675 a certain William Cadowgan left to Upper Parish in Nansemond County land and stock the income from which was "to be disposed of, by the churchwardens and vestry of the said parish, towards the maintenance of the poor, and other charitable uses." In 1752 the Assembly allowed the vestry to sell the property as it then existed, and provided "that the money arising by the sale of the said lands, and the said stock, shall be by them applied, for and towards erecting a house for the reception of the poor of the said parish."[30] In the vestry record for the meeting held November 4, 1754, appears the following entry concerning the parish workhouse which was constructed:

The house Built for the reception of the Poor of the Parrish Being now finished According to Agreement Is Received by the Vestry And Persuant to the Act of the Assembly for that Purpose Made and provided . . . it is ordered that the Church wardens of this Parrish at Christmas next or some Convenient time soon after Convei into the Said house all the Poor persons that now is or hereafter shall be Maintained at the Parrish Expense there to be supported. . . . And it is frither ordered that Samuel Wallis then Be Admitted into the Said House as Overseer and Master and that he take Care of the Furniture and Provisions Which shall be provided for the said poor. And furthermore that he Teach eight poor Children which are to be sent into the Said House by the Churchwardens to Read Rite etc. For all which service The Said Samuel Wallis to have and Receive from this Parrish Annually the Sum of Twenty Pounds Current Money, His own Children Accommodated and Liberty To take in and School ten children besides the Poor Accordin as he Can Agree with there Parents, etc. During the time he shall be continued . . .

The record of the Upper Parish vestry meetings for the period following 1755 show that the poorhouse school was in operation until 1759, when it was discontinued. In 1755 Wallis received his twenty pounds, but his salary for 1756 was reduced to ten pounds, as shown in the following order:

That Samuel Wallis be Continued in the poorhouse the ensueing year at Ten pounds Current Money and that there is a woman as an assistant Imploy'd when occasion Require by the Church Wardens and that he have Liberty to take in and School Fifteen Children besides our Poor them not Exceeding Eight.

The master was to be allowed to increase the number of pay

[30]Hening, VI, 266, 518.

pupils as an inducement for him to continue to teach the parish children at the reduced salary. In the minutes for the meeting in June, 1756, appears the only record of a dependent child being placed in the poorhouse for schooling: "That the Daughter Margaret hall be put in the almshouse There to be School'd." In 1756 Wallis received his ten pounds "for keeping School, etc.," and in 1757 and 1758 he was paid as "Teacher at ye poor house." In the record of January 1, 1759 the following entry appears:

Whereas Mr. Samuel Wallice hath been Imployd some time past by the Vestry of this parish to take care of the poor house and to educate the poor children of the parish and it appearing that a sufficient Number of children cannot be got to be educated In the said house and that Continueing the said Mr. Wallice will be Running the Parish to expense without having the Desired Good efect it is therefore ordered that the Church wardens of this parrish Do account with and Discharge the said Mr. Wallice on the Seventeenth day of this Instant being the end of the year of his said service and that they employ some sober careful person to Look after the said House.[31]

In 1763 the parish was debtor "To Samuel Wallis for John Orans Schooling and Wood 2-8-2"; in 1769 he was paid for "schooling some poor children" six pounds; and in 1770 "for schooling several poor children" he was paid 4£, 17s., 6p.

The above extracts from the vestry records make it appear that there was not a sufficient number of dependent children in the parish to make it worth while to maintain the school in the workhouse. Poor parents probably preferred to keep their children at home rather than have them placed in the institution. It would seem as though poor children residing near the workhouse might have attended the school at the same time living in their homes. There is, however, no suggestion of a desire on the part of the parents for such an arrangement or of a recognition on the part of the vestry that this plan might be followed. The fact that the master was allowed to teach private pay pupils in the school as partial compensation for his work indicates that the vestry did not think that association with the poorhouse would be looked upon by people in the community as objectionable, and the fact that the master was allowed to increase the number of pay pupils from ten to fifteen shows that he must have had a number of them in his school. In spite of the fact that the cost of educating parish children was provided for entirely or in large part by a gift to the parish the plan did not succeed. As suggested, the reason seems to have been in the

[31]Upper Parish, Nansemond County, MS. Vestry Minutes.

lack of a keen interest on the part of the vestrymen, who could have made some adaptations, and in a lack of a strong desire on the part of the poorer people to have their children educated. In any case, the Upper Parish workhouse school, which was the only institution of the kind established in Virginia in the colonial period, failed under circumstances which apparently were relatively favorable.

CHAPTER V

PARISH APPRENTICESHIP

ENGLISH PRECEDENTS IN PARISH APPRENTICESHIP

During the seventeenth and eighteenth centuries poor law apprenticeship was used in England as the chief means of caring for dependent children and relieving the public from charges for their support.[1] The indenture under which the children were bound was essentially the same as for industrial apprenticeship,[2] but the intention back of the law governing the practice was to provide maintenance and oversight rather than education.

ye meaning of ye statute was not for the education of boys in arts but for charity to keep ym and relieve ym from turning to roguery and idleness, so a man's house was, as it were, a Hospital in yt case, rather than a shop of trade.[3]

Even though it had been intended to make regular trade education a part of the plan, the early age at which the children were apprenticed and the oversupply of labor would have interfered effectively with an attempt to require it of the masters. That the overseers of the poor were concerned primarily with relieving the parish from responsibility of support rather than with the provision of training or proper bringing up is shown by Dunlop[4] and by Burn in his *History of the Poor Laws*, written in 1764. Burn said that the overseers understood their duty to be,

To maintain their poor as cheap as possibly they can at all events; . . .to bind out poor children apprentice no matter to whom or to what trade, but to take special care that the master live in another parish.[5]

The attitude of the poor law officials is shown by the fact that the larger share of the children were bound to husbandry and house-

---

[1] Dunlop, *English Apprenticeship and Child Labor*, p. 248.
[2] *Poor Laws, or the Laws and Statutes relating to the Settling, Maintenance, and Employment of the Poor* (1727), p. 10.
[3] Dunlop, p. 252. A court decision in the case of the gentry of Sheffield and its environs who tried to establish immunity from taking poor apprentices.
[4] Dunlop, p. 256.
[5] Burn, *History of the Poor Laws*, p. 211.

wifery with the understanding that they should serve as general help in return for their livelihood.[6]

All persons were required to take poor apprentices "who by their profession or manner of living, have occasion to use servants."[7] People of the better class in character and occupation objected to taking them, and they usually accepted them only because of the fine attached to refusal, even though a premium was paid and boys were bound until twenty-four. It was early decided that the justices had power to coerce those who refused:

and if any such Master shall refuse to take such Apprentice (according to their Discretion) [that is the overseers'] so to him appointed, the said Justices may bind such Master over to the next General Gaol-delivery, there to answer his Default. And this was the Direction of Sir *Henry* Mountagne Knight, Chief Justice of the King's Bench at Cambridge Assises, Anno Dom. 1618.[8]

An act of Parliament passed in 1696 set at ten pounds the fine for refusal to take an apprentice.[9] Persons who were willing to accept parish children usually were not of a type to make satisfactory masters, and the system was characterized by much abuse of the children.[10] William Bailey, writing in 1758, said,

The present Method of putting out poor children apprentices, is very well known to be attended with great Inconveniences, as it lays an Incumbrance on Estates, and Families. Few of those poor children now serve out their Time, and many of them are driven, by Neglect or Cruelty, into such Immoralities as to frequently render them the objects of publick Justice. Many of those who take Parish apprentices are so inhuman, as to regard only the pecuniary Consideration, and having once received that, they, by ill Usage and Severity often drive the poor Creatures from them.[11]

Some of the children no doubt were placed with masters who gave attention to their trade training,[12] but as a whole, English poor law apprenticeship should not be looked upon as having been an effective educational device and should hardly be considered to have been apprenticeship in the proper meaning of the word.[13] Partly in recognition of the unfortunate conditions under which poor apprentices served and the careless manner of their bringing up, there was made in the eighteenth century workhouses and charity schools a more or

---

[6]Dalton, *Country Justice*, p. 85.
[7]Burn, Richard, *The Justice of the Peace and Parish Officer* (1772), I, p. 63.
[8]Dalton, *Country Justice*, p. 166.
[9]8 and 9 Wm. III, cap. 30.
[10]Dunlop, *English Apprenticeship*, pp. 256–59.
[11]Bailey, Wm., *A Treatise on the Better Employment and More Comfortable Support of the Poor in Workhouses* (1758), p. 5.
[12]Leonard, *English Poor Relief*, p. 226.
[13]Dunlop, p. 249.

less successful attempt to instruct parish children in reading, writing, and the catechism before they reached the age to be bound out.

The general statute under which pauper children were bound out in England in the seventeenth and eighteenth centuries was the Elizabethan poor law of 1601,[14] the apprenticeship provisions of which were not repealed until 1814. This made the parish churchwardens and the overseers of the poor the poor law officials, and gave to them the duty of apprenticing the children whose parents they might think not "fit or able to keep or maintain them." The law stipulated that they might raise "competent sums of money" by parish levy for premiums to be paid the masters taking the children, and it required that in apprenticing a child they should secure the assent of two justices of the peace.[15] The custom seems to have been for the justices to register their assent by use of the following form filled in and copied at the bottom of the indenture, although sometimes the statement of concurrence was incorporated in the indenture:

We T. L. and M. T., two of his majesty's Justices of the Peace for the County Aforesaid, do hereby declare our Consent to the putting forth of the abovesaid L. M. Apprentice to the said J. K. according to the intent and meaning of the Indenture above written.[16]

Probably in the ordinary course of events the action of the justices was purely formal, but in the many cases where legal questions arose in the administration of the law the justices took the responsibility.

In summary, the English scheme of pauper apprenticeship with which the American colonists were familiar was not primarily an educational arrangement, but rather a system of compulsory support and guardianship of children administered under the supervision of the county justices by the parish poor law officers who had the right to use parish funds to partially compensate the masters.

PARISH APPRENTICESHIP IN VIRGINIA

The English system of compulsory apprenticeship was continued

---

[14] 43 Elizabeth, cap. 2.

[15] The granting of the power to levy taxes to provide for apprenticeship premiums which was first given in the law of 1601 may be considered to be the first step taken in England toward public support of education, but the general lack of an educational element in the scheme and the dominance of the poor support motive raise a question as to whether the taxation provided for should be considered to have been educational taxation. Whether in fact it was the first step toward public support can best be determined by a study of the sequence of events in the later development.

[16] *Poor Laws* or *The Laws & Statutes relating to the Settling, Maintenance & Employment of the Poor* (1727), p. 11; Dalton, *Country Justice*, p. 447.

in Virginia but it was used in the colony as a means of education as well as of support. The statutes distinguished three classes of children who were subject to forced apprenticeship: poor orphans,[17] children who were not being brought up properly because of the poverty,[18] disordered lives, or carelessness of their parents,[19] and illegitimate children.[20] Before 1769 the law required that bastard children should be bound out as servants,[21] but in that year they were put upon the same basis as other poor children and apprenticed under the same indenture.[22] It was assumed or directly stated in all of the apprenticeship laws that training in a trade should be given, but the first prescription of instruction in reading and writing for children of any of the classes mentioned above was made in an enactment of 1705 which dealt with the apprenticing of poor orphans.[23] Schooling was not required of masters of children apprenticed because of the poverty or neglect of their parents until 1727.

In the various statutes dealing with forced apprenticeship there are four objects indicated: the improvement of industry by the training of skilled workers,[24] the reduction of the amount of poverty and vagabondage,[25] the better bringing up of otherwise uncared for children,[26] and relief from public responsibility for support.[27] Con-

---

[17]Hening, I, 416 (1656). The laws referred to here were not the only ones making the distinctions between the classes of children. The statute of 1656 provided that orphans were to be bound to a manual trade "if the estate will not reach to a free education."

[18]Hening, I, 336 (1646); II, 298 (1672).

[19]Hening, IV, 212 (1727); VI, 32 (1748). It was not until the passage of the law of 1748 that proper bringing up specifically included due care of the education of children. The law of 1727 was as follows: "That if it should happen, that the parent or parents of any child or children, upon due proof before the court of the county wherein such parent or parents inhabit, shall be adjudged incapable of supporting and bringing up such child or children, by reason of his, her, or their idle, dissolute, and disorderly course of life, or that they neglect to take due care of the education and instruction of such child or children, in christian principles, that then it shall and may be lawful upon certificate from the said court, to and for the churchwardens of the said parish, where such child or children shall inhabit to bind out, or put to service or apprentice, such child or children, for such time or term, and under such covenants, as hath been usual and customary, or the law directs in the case of orphan children."

[20]Hening, I, 438 (1662); III, 87 (1691). Mulattoes were also distinguished, but they may be considered as illegitimates.

[21]Hening, III, 87.

[22]Hening, VIII, 374–77 (1769).

[23]Hening, III, 375 (1705): "And the master of every such orphan shall be obliged to teach him to read and write."

[24]Hening, I, 336 (1646); IV, 482 (1736).

[25]Hening, II, 298 (1672), An "Act for Suppressing vagabonds and disposeing of poore children to trades."

[26]Hening, IV, 212 (1727).

[27]Hening, III, 375 (1705): "And if the estate of any orphan be of so small a

sidering the laws as a whole it cannot be said that any one of the objects sought was dominant in the minds of the legislators. It seems, however, that as time went on there was an increasing interest in the welfare of the children concerned. This is suggested by the addition of educational requirements and the placing of illegitimates on the same basis as other children.

The duty of apprenticing poor orphans was in law in the hands of the county justices,[28] while the binding out of bastards as servants or apprentices was given to the parish wardens.[29] The apprenticing of children of poor or careless parents was assigned to the justices until a law of 1727 delegated the work to the wardens acting "upon certificate" from the county court.[30] Before 1727, however, the wardens participated in the work of apprenticing children of parents not able to bring them up by submitting to the courts the names of children subject to the law.[31] Since we are primarily concerned with parish activity in education we should note that after 1727 the wardens had the larger share of the responsibility for carrying out the laws of compulsory apprenticeship, although the binding out of orphans and the general supervision of the system was left to the county courts.[32] The certification provided for in the law of 1727 corresponded to the "assent" prescribed in the English law of 1601, although it was not the custom as in England to register the consent in the indenture. Probably it was the practice when the court was a party to the procedure for the wardens to take the names of children and proposed masters to the justices, who then approved the proposed disposition of the children by an order. In view of this a record showing children bound out by the wardens "upon order of the court" does not mean that the justices initiated the proceeding or had more than a formal part in binding out the children.

The scheme of forced apprenticeship which is outlined in the statutes of colonial Virginia is in brief as follows. In general all children whose education was not properly provided for by parents

---

value, that no person will maintain him for the profits thereof. . . ." etc. In a statute of 1769 which was concerned with the apprenticing of illegitimate children, there is complaint that the laws were insufficient for indemnifying parishes "from the great charges frequently arising from children begotten out of lawful matrimony" (Hening, VII, 374).

[28]Hening, II, 298.
[29]Hening, III, 87 (1691); VIII, 374.
[30]Hening, IV, 212.
[31]Hening, II, 298 (1672).
[32]Hening, V, 452 (1748). There were earlier laws which had the same general import.

or guardians were to be apprenticed. At first only trade training was required of masters but in the first part of the eighteenth century instruction in reading and writing also came to be required, except for girls. In the seventeenth century the execution of the laws was in the hands of the county court, and the court continued to have responsibility for apprenticing orphans. Early in the eighteenth century the parish wardens were given the duty of binding out all except poor orphans, although according to law the court shared in the work by giving an order or certificate to the wardens in the case of each child apprenticed. If the law had been strictly followed the study of parish activity in apprenticeship would be limited to an examination of the work of the wardens acting in conjunction with the court in binding out children other than orphans in the period after 1727, in which year the duty of apprenticing children was first given them. It will be shown, however, that the law was not closely followed.

The vestries never had a duty with regard to apprenticeship assigned to them by statute, and yet the vestry books show that in the period which they cover it was a common practice for them to bind out poor children of the three types distinguished in law, including, occasionally, orphans with property. The assumption by the vestries of the charge of binding out dependent children naturally proceeded from their having general charge of the care of the poor, and from the fact that the wardens were appointed by them from among their own number and were responsible to them. In the vestry meetings the cases of persons partially or entirely dependent upon the parish for support, or likely to become so, were brought up for action, and in the cases of poor children, whether orphans or not, there were the alternatives of providing support or binding them out. There are many illustrations in the vestry books showing how in the natural course of events the apprenticing of poor children fell into the vestry's hands. Following are typical cases:

Ordered that the Child Widow Bass now hath nursing for ye parish be bound out by indenture to ye aforesaid widdow Bass by the Churchwardens (Bristol Parish, 1720).

Whereas George Peirson ye son of George Peirson decd has bin from time past a burden to ye parish Henry Bray prefering to ease ye parish and the said child off (from being any charge for the future) Order is by this present vestry that the Church wardens bind him out to Henry Bray with pd come to the age of one and twenty years (Petsworth Parish, 1692).

Upon the petition of Eliz. Glidewell that she is a poor widow and not able to take care of her children desires that her son Robt. Glidewell be bound to Tho Clemmon as the law directs Tis granted (Bristol Parish, 1729).

Ordered that Francis, Agnes, Thomas, and Averillah, children of Mary Gerrard, Widdow, be bound out by the church wardens (St. Paul's Parish, 1736).

To Mrs. Abagail Richardson, for Mary and susanna Jeffs, children of Sarah Jeffs, in full for the Time she hath kept them, and to indemnify the Parish from all charges for keeping and bringing them up the said children for the time to come, they being now bound apprentices to her (Henrico, 1771).

That the vestry commonly assumed responsibility for the binding out of poor children is indicated in Hugh Jones' *Present State of Virginia*, written in 1722:

For where there is a numerous Family of Poor Children the Vestry takes care to bind them out Apprentices, till they are able to maintain themselves by their own labor.[33]

Whenever the wardens bound out a child upon vestry order, the indenture was probably given to the vestry clerk for preservation along with other official papers. If the clerk was especially careful, or if the vestry required it of him, he copied the indenture into the permanent record, but the indenture was a relatively lengthy, formal paper, and as long as the original was kept there was no real necessity of copying it. After the expiration of the term of service to which the child was bound there was no good reason for keeping the original, and so we have the contracts kept only in those cases where a copy was made. In the Petsworth Parish vestry book there are evidences showing that the vestry was unusually conscientious in its work, and here we find that the indenture was ordinarily recorded in the body of the vestry record following the order for apprenticing a child. In Fredericksville Parish in Louisa County the vestry required the clerk to record the indentures of children they ordered to be apprenticed in a special book devoted to the purpose, but they paid him for his work, as for instance in 1770: "Dr. to ditto [the clerk] for recording four indentures—120 [pounds of tobacco]." It is only in the case of Fredericksville Parish that we have an apparently complete record for a considerable period of years of indentures binding out children whose apprenticeship was ordered by the vestry, but for the reasons which have been indicated little significance should be attached to the lack of similar records in other parishes.

Where it was customary after 1727 for the wardens to apprentice children "upon certificate" from the county court instead of upon

[33]Jones Hugh, *Present State of Virginia*, p. 54.

order of the vestry, the probability is that they gave the indenture to the vestry clerk just as they did where the work was done under direction from the vestry. In this case, however, after the disposal of the original indenture at the end of the period of service no evidence would remain except where it was the practice to make a copy for preservation. And since the binding out was not ordered by the vestry, the clerk would seldom record it as a part of the official vestry business. It is possible that in such case it was the more or less common practice for the clerk to record the indenture in a special book, although none has been found. In one parish, however, it was the consistent policy for the clerk to copy in the back of the vestry book the indentures of children apprenticed upon order of the court. This was in Dettingen Parish in Prince William County.

The chief problem in the study of compulsory apprenticeship is the determination of the number of children who were provided for in the system. It will make the solution of this problem simpler if at first attention be confined to the period after 1727 in which, for the reasons above indicated, we may assume that the actual indenturing of poor children was done by the wardens either upon vestry or court order. For this period there is an adequate number of vestry books upon which to base conclusions, whereas there is not for the earlier time. If a correct judgment as to numbers is made for the last fifty years of the colonial period, we may make a sufficiently trustworthy inference for the time preceding.

Following is a list of the parishes whose vestry books have been examined, with the number of cases of apprenticeship recorded in each case in the period from 1726 to 1776 or for a period within these limits for which we have what is apparently a complete record.

Parish	Period	Cases	Average Yearly Number
Albemarle, Sussex	1741–1776	0	—
Antrim, Halifax	1752–1770	0	—
Blissland, New Kent	1726–1776		
Bristol, Prince George	1726–1749	32	1.45
Christ Church, Lancaster	1739–1776	0	—
Christ Church, Middlesex	1726–1776	0	—
Cumberland, Lunenburg	1747–1776	0	—
Dettingen, Pr. William	1751–1776	67	2.6
Elizabeth City, Elizabeth City	1751–1776	2	.08
Frederick, Frederick	1764–1776	0	—
Fredericksville, Louisa	1742–1776	61	1.8
Henrico, Henrico	1730–1773	3	.05

King William, Henrico	1727–1750	0	—
Kingston, Mathews	1727–1776	1	—
Linhaven, Lower Norfolk	1727–1776	0	—
Petsworth, Gloucester	1727–1776	24	.48
St. George, Spotsylvania	1727–1776	0	—
St. James, Goochland	1744–1776	1	—
St, Mark's, Culpeper	1730–1776	2	—
St. Patrick's, Prince Edward	1755–1774	0	—
St. Paul's, Hanover	1727–1738	16	1.3
St. Peter's, New Kent	1727–1759	3	—
Shelbourne, Loudon	1771–1776	0	—
Stratton Major, King and Queen	1729–1776	16	.34
Truro, Fairfax	1737–1740	11	2.7
Upper Parish, Nansemond	1744–1776	0	—
Wicomico, Westmoreland	1727–1776	0	—

If it should be assumed that for the parishes and the periods indicated we have a complete record of all the children apprenticed by the wardens either upon court or vestry order, the conclusion would be that an altogether inconsiderable number of poor children were apprenticed. But the wide differences between the parishes, in some cases between those in adjoining counties, make it certain that the record for some is incomplete. In some cases where there is no evidence of apprenticeship it is likely that the wardens apprenticed children without vestry intervention, and that the indentures were not preserved or recorded. In view of these considerations, attention may be limited to several of the parishes in which the largest number of children were bound out and for which the record for a considerable period seems complete. Even in these cases conclusions can be only approximately correct.

The Bristol Parish vestry book covers the period from 1720 to 1789. In 1720 the vestry ordered the apprenticing of two orphans and the binding out to service of one illegitimate child. In most of the years following down to 1748 similar action was taken. In 1748 two bastard children were bound to apprenticeship "by an order of the court of Prince George County," and in 1749 it was ordered "That the church wardens petition the court to bind out Ann the daughter of Robert Hudson." In these two years no other cases are recorded, and in the years following there is no further reference to apprenticeship. Why the court should have desired to take over the work of ordering the apprenticing of poor children after it had been for several decades in the hands of the vestry is difficult to see, but it is apparently because the court took the duty that there is no further reference to apprenticeship in the parish records. The Prince George County order books for the period are destroyed so that it is impossible to determine any of the facts in the matter by means of them. Whatever may have been the cause of the change of policy, the important question from the standpoint of an attempt to determine the number of children apprenticed in the parish is as to whether the vestry in the period from 1727 to 1749 took practically the sole responsibility in ordering the binding out of poor motherless or fatherless children, the children of poor or negligent parents, and illegitimates, or whether there was a division of the work with the court ordering the binding out of children of the same types.

The Bristol vestry record suggests that from 1720 to 1748 the vestry was the recognized authority in the parish for the indenturing of poor children of all classes, and that practically all who were provided for by this means were bound out by the vestry. The following typical cases from the vestry book serve as evidence.

Mr. Theo. Bott haveing an orphant boy bound to him by his mother desires the same may be confirmed by this vestry (1720).

Upon the petition of Eliz. Lett It is ordered that James Lett her son now being at Tho. Gregories be by the Church wardens bound unto Daniell nance and his wife untill the said James come to lawful age (1722).

Upon the motion of Daniel Jackson That John Pucket is run away and left one of his children by name Eliz. pucket prayes that ye said child be bound to him and his heirs as the law directs. Tis granted (1728).

Upon the petition of Eliz. Glidewell that she is a poor widow and not able to take care of her children desires that her son Robt. Glidewell be bound to Tho. Clemon as the law directs Tis granted (1729).

Ordered that Willm Bleik (alias Pride) be bound to Willm Pride supposed to be his father (1731).

Ordered that the children of William Stow dec'd be bound out by the vestry as the law directs (1731).

Ordered that Mary Blys Child be bound to Peter Gill born the 17th Feb. 1729 Named Joshua Irby (1731).

Ordered that Henry Voden assigne Eliz. Brown an orphan girl over to Wm. Pirkason (1735).

William Eppes and Theodorick Bland Churchwardens of the parish put Instance Hall (son of John Hall deceased) an apprentice to Wm. Sturdivant as the law directs to learn the trade of shoemaking (1747–8).

The variety of cases, the apprenticing of orphans, the continuous record, the petitions to the vestry, and the lack of reference to the justices as officials binding out children point to the conclusion that in the period from 1720 to 1748 the vestry was the body which took the responsibility for ordering the apprenticing of poor children in the parish.

Limiting attention to the period from 1727 to 1748, we find that thirty-two children, or an average of about 1.5 each year, were apprenticed in Bristol Parish.[34] The significance of this number, however, can only be seen by comparing it with the total number of white children in the parish who were of proper age to be apprenticed, and this number cannot be determined accurately. The facts as they existed in 1740 may be approximated and taken as typical for the period. The white children born in Bristol Parish in 1740, 1741, and 1742 numbered 51, 81, and 76 respectively.[35] If sixty births each year be taken as normal for some years preceding 1740, and if it be assumed that ten per cent of all children born in the parish died, there were in 1740 somewhat over five hundred white children in the parish who were more than three years old and less than fourteen.[36] At the same time there were, on the basis 1.5 as the average number apprenticed each year, perhaps fifteen children, or three per cent of all, who had been apprenticed under the poor law. In view of the fact that there were relatively many poor people in the colony at the time,[37] we should be justified in concluding that among

---

[34]In this period there were also twenty illegitimate children, mainly mulattoes, "bound to serve as the law directs." At this time the law directed that bastards should be bound to service.

[35]*Bristol Parish Register.* Bristol Parish is taken for detailed study because the vestry book and register have been published, allowing more careful examination than can readily be made in the case of other parishes. The number of births was somewhat greater than that indicated above for the register of names beginning with D, E, and F is missing for the years preceding 1745, and probably some births in lower class families were not registered. Of 100 illegitimate children which are shown by the register, the record of fines, or the record of apprenticeship to have been born in Bristol Parish between 1719 and 1770 only 51 have their births recorded in the register.

[36]In industrial apprenticeship the age for binding out children was thirteen or fourteen, but in the system of poor law apprenticeship in Virginia children were usually bound out at an earlier age, often as infants.

[37]No adequate study of the number of poor people in colonial Virginia has been made, but it is clear that there were many of them. The ratio between the number of dependent poor receiving public aid and the number of tithables was, according to a rough estimate based on the vestry records, 20 to 1200. This takes no account of the vagabond class or of the poor who got along without parish aid. While the statutes of the colony are not by themselves a safe basis for judgments as to actual facts of any sort, the following extracts from the laws are a kind of proof that there were many poor.

A law of 1672 (Hening, II, 298) stated that the neglect of certain English statutes "hath encouraged and much encreased the number of vagabonds idle and dissolute persons." In an act of 1727 (Hening, IV, 208) there is complaint that idle and disorderly persons able to work "strole from one county to another, neglecting to labor," and that vagabonds "run from their habitations and

the ninety-seven per cent not apprenticed there were a great many poor children who were not receiving an education either of a trade or school type. That this conclusion is correct is shown in a description of conditions as they existed in the parish a few years later.

In 1755 a committee composed of members of the vestries of the neighboring parishes of Bristol, Martins Brandon, and Bath made a report to their respective vestries concerning a proposal to establish a school in connection with a workhouse.[38] The plan was proposed by the Bristol Parish representatives, of whom Theodorick Bland, the leading man in the community, was one. The part of the report which is descriptive of conditions is as follows:

This committee having taken under their most consideration the unhappy and indeed miserable circumstances of the many poor orphans and other poor children, inhabitants of the said parishes, whose parents are utterly unable to give them any education and being desirous. . .that such poor children should be brought up in a religious, virtuous and industrious course of life, have resolved earnestly to recommend it to their respective vestries that they should join in a petition to the general Assembly. . .(Bristol Parish vestry book, pp. 165–66)

The above description of the situation is very significant not only as an indication of the bad condition educationally of the large number of children not apprenticed, but also as in effect a recognition of the inefficacy of poor apprenticeship as an educational means.[39] The law definitely provided that "the many poor orphans and other poor children" mentioned should be apprenticed, properly brought up by masters, and given instruction in a trade and in reading and writing.[40] If it had been the consistent policy for the masters of

leave either wives or children without suitable means of support." The following is an introductory paragraph in an enactmnet of 1755 (Hening VI, 475).

"WHEREAS the number of poor people hath of late years much increased throughout this colony . . . and it will be the most proper method for their maintenance, and for the prevention of great mischiefs arising from such numbers of unemployed poor. to provide houses for their reception and employment, . . ."

[38]See above, p. 64.

[39]While no other contemporary description of the condition of poor children in Virginia has been found, there is a similar statement with reference to Maryland where there were corresponding poor apprenticeship laws and somewhat the same social conditions. There is a certain amount of confirmation of the conclusions reached with respect to Virginia in this statement. Rev. Thomas Bacon, who at the middle of the 18th century undertook the establishment of a charity work school in Talbot County, Maryland, preached a sermon in London in the endeavor to get contributions to help in carrying out the project. He said in the sermon,

"God only knows, the great necessity of such a work in this province, where education is hardly to be attained at any rate by the children of the poor, much greater than can be apprehended from the general complaint, or even discovered by the particular inquiry of such as are put upon it by the duties of their station." (Steiner, *History of Education in Maryland*, p. 34)

[40]Hening, IV, 208; V, 451.

children apprenticed to follow the law either voluntarily or because of
the oversight of the court which the law provided for, there would
have been no reason for the complaint in the report or for an attempt
to put a new plan into operation.   If the disobedience had been
merely a temporary lapse and if the system of apprenticeship had
not been under the conditions inherently unsatisfactory as an educational means, the members of the vestry, who were the most in-
fluential men in the community, could readily have brought about a
reform.   Mr. Bland, for instance, was a member of the vestry, clerk
of the county court, and a member of the House of Burgesses.

It may be stated here that while it would be possible to give too
great significance to the statement in the Bristol Parish vestry book
as an indication of the educational conditions with respect to the
poor in Virginia in the eighteenth century, it is certainly the best
evidence bearing on the subject.   It shows the working of the scheme
of apprenticeship rather than the theory as expressed in the law or as
it may be inferred from the study of individual cases of children
bound out.   It also shows the futility of an attempt to attach importance to the detailed provisions and minor amendments of the
law.

How is the state of affairs described by the committee on the
workhouse school to be related to the fact that it was the consistent
policy of the Bristol Parish vestry over a long period to apprentice
one or two children each year?   The probability is that the authorities
confined their attention to the cases of children who were dependent
on the public for support or were likely to become so, and that
ordinarily other children of the poor were not apprenticed.

In Dettingen Parish sixty-seven children, or an average of two or
three each year, were apprenticed between 1751 and 1776.   The
record of apprenticeship in this parish is in the form of indentures made
by the wardens "upon order of the county court" and copied in the
back of the vestry book.   The activity of the vestry was confined to
ordering the binding to service of nine illegitimate children in the
period from 1745 to 1753.   After 1753 the court seems to have taken
entire charge of the binding out of children both to service and to
apprenticeship.   The indentures made out before 1765 were not
recorded in the year in which they were drawn up, but were copied
mixed in order of time—1764, 1751, 1760, 1752, etc.   Apparently it
was the custom before 1763 for the clerk to keep the original indentures along with other parish papers, but in that year the clerk

was required to copy them, and ordinarily thereafter the order of time was followed. The fact that all the apprenticing was done upon order of the court, that all classes of poor children were bound out by the wardens upon court order, and that there are enough cases over a long period to show a consistent policy makes it reasonably certain that we have in the record an account of all poor children who were apprenticed under the poor law in the parish.

The total number of recorded cases of apprenticeship in Dettingen Parish is larger than for any other parish, the average of 2.6 per year is greater than for any other, except for Truro Parish for a short time; and considering the number of tithables, of whom there were 1287 in 1760,[41] the relative number of children apprenticed was more than twice that in Bristol Parish. One explanation of this fact is that there were relatively many poor people and young orphans in the parish.[42] Another explanation is that Dumfries, which was in Dettingen Parish, was during the latter part of the colonial period an important center of trade so that the possibilities of apprenticeship were more readily realized than in most of the other parishes. Bishop Meade says that Dumfries was "once the mart of that part of Virginia, . . . the abode of wealthy merchants from Scotland."[43] However, the number of poor children apprenticed, considering the number of poor people in the parish, is not much if any greater than would be called for by the rule that dependents should be bound out.

In Fredericksville Parish sixty-one children were apprenticed in the period from 1742 to 1776, an average of 1.8 per year. The case of this parish is similar to that of Dettingen in that there was a relatively large number of children bound out and that the record was in the form of indentures, but the apprenticing here was done by the wardens upon vestry order instead of upon court order. Children other than those for whom we have record may have been apprenticed by court order, but the evidence indicating that the work was done by the vestry is of the same type as in Bristol Parish.

The Truro Parish vestry book has no record of apprenticeship except for the years 1737 to 1740, and here it is in the form of indentures copied in with the vestry minutes. No doubt parish children were bound out before and after these dates and we may assume that there was not much variation from 2.7 each year which

---

[41]MS. Vestry Book, 1760.
[42]For instance, see page 77 in the parish vestry book.
[43]Meade, *Old Churches and Families of Virginia*, II, 209.

was the average number apprenticed in the period from 1737 to
to 1740. This leads to the same conclusion as that reached in the
consideration of the other parishes—that dependent children were
bound out.

In the case of Petsworth Parish the record shows that the vestry
apprenticed children of all types distinguished in law, and that they
exercised an unusual interest in the children, sometimes paying
premiums and as early as 1700 requiring of the master three years
schooling.[44] It is impossible to determine whether the vestry
ordered the apprenticing of all poor children who were bound out in
the parish, but there are the following indications that they did.
The vestry regularly ordered the apprenticeship of poor orphans,
which in law was a duty of the court, and they occasionally bound out
orphans with property; they demanded three years of schooling
before the law required it; they sometimes paid premiums to masters
for taking children; and the record shows a continuous policy. The
premium in cases of children without property was paid by the parish
as the institution responsible for the care of the poor, and it is unlikely that the court would order the apprenticing of children when
the payment of the premium was customary—thus requiring the
vestry to make an outlay of parish money. In Petsworth Parish
the educational motive is more apparent than in any other parish,
but the relatively small number of cases, an average of .48 per year,
shows that this purpose was not strong enough to make the vestry
look upon apprenticeship as a means of giving education to any
large share of the poor children of the parish. The motive which
was probably the fundamental one in this parish as in the others is
suggested by a record made in 1721. The wardens were required to
bind out an illegitimate child "as soon as possible they can gitt any-
body to take it off them."[45]

Except in the cases of the parishes which have been considered
above, the extant records, in each case covering part or all of the
period from 1727 to 1776, show few or no cases of apprenticeship.
But it is reasonable to assume that because of the desire to relieve
the public from charges for support the policy of binding out the
dependent children was generally followed. The lack of records in
some parishes may mean that the wardens acted upon their own

[44]The court record of Gloucester County in which Petsworth Parish was located has been destroyed.
[45]Petsworth Parish MS. Vestry Book, p. 109.

initiative, that is without vestry order, and that the indentures were not kept after the expiration of the terms of service. In other parishes the practice was probably like that in Dettingen where the court took charge of certificating the binding out of dependent children. It may be that here the original indentures were not preserved and that if books for recording the contracts were used they were lost after the end of the colonial period. We may be sure, however, that the more seriously apprenticeship was considered in any parish and the larger the number of cases the greater the probability that a parish record of orders or indentures was kept and the greater the likelihood that some evidence would be preserved to the present, whether the wardens acted independently or upon vestry or court order. If we were considering the period before 1727, in which year the wardens were made by law the agents for apprenticing poor children other than orphans, we might explain the lack of evidence of poor apprenticeship in the parish records in some cases, and the small number taking all into consideration, by assuming that the work was done almost entirely by the county courts; but in view of the facts which have been brought out this does not serve as an explanation after 1727. It may be assumed that the county courts in the period after 1727, as well as before, followed the law fairly closely and apprenticed dependent orphans, although the assumption of some of the work by the vestries and the statement in the Bristol Parish vestry book to the effect that "many poor orphans" were not bound out make it seem doubtful.

Heretofore attention has been confined mainly to the period after 1727. With regard to the earlier period, in which the courts were legally responsible for apprenticing all classes of poor children except illegitimates, it may be said that there is little reason for thinking that a larger share of poor children were bound out than in the later period, and the probability is that, considering the growth of enlightenment and the improvement in the conditions of living, the relative number apprenticed was greater in the latter part of the colonial period than in the earlier. It may be, however, that the inadequacy of the system became more apparent as time went on.[46]

The conclusion that ordinarily only the children who were dependents were bound out in compulsory apprenticeship means that the laws providing for neglected children of poor parents were not

[46]For a discussion of apprenticeship in the seventeenth century see Bruce, *Institutional History of Virginia*, I, 311–14.

generally enforced. This calls for an explanation. In the first place it should be understood that the laws of colonial Virginia are not to be depended upon as indications of actual practices. Many laws seem to have been enacted as an expression of desire on the part of the legislators without proper consideration being given to custom or to conditions under which they were to be carried out. There are many illustrations of the futility of legislation. In Chapter IV it has been shown that the laws dealing with workhouses and the improvement of the woolen industry were of little or no effect. As another illustration we have the laws dealing with minor morals and religious observances.[47] The fact that the laws which provided most adequately for the education in apprenticeship of the children of poor or neglectful parents, that is those of 1727 and 1748, merely gave power to the wardens and courts without requiring them to act, is a partial explanation of their lack of effect.

However serious were the intentions of the legislators, there were several factors in the situation which effectively interfered with the execution of the laws. As has been shown, a chief motive in enacting the statutes of apprenticeship was the desire to add to the number of skilled workers and thus in a measure raise industry from its low state. But the elements in the situation making the condition of manufactures unsatisfactory also interfered with the development of apprenticeship, and no doubt made parents and the local authorities look upon it with disfavor as a means of education. The following description of industrial conditions and practices at the middle of the colonial period shows how the development of an artisan class was discouraged and indicates that those who were directly concerned with apprenticeship could not have thought of it as offering much advantage to those subject to the law.

For want of Towns, Markets, and Money, there is but little Encouragement for Tradesmen and Artificers, and therefore little Choice of them, and their Labour very dear in the country. Then a great deal of Tradesman's Time being necessarily spent in going and coming to and from his Work, in dispers'd County Plantations, and his Pay being generally in straggling Parcels of Tobacco, the Collection whereof costs about 10 *per cent*, and the best of this Pay coming but once a Year, so that he cannot turn his Hand frequently with a small stock, as Tradesmen do in *England* and elsewhere, all this occasions the Dearth of all

---

[47]It is possible to show in a number of ways the common non-observance of some of the laws dealing with morals. For evidence in the laws themselves see Hening, III,168; III, 205; IV, 244.

Tradesmen's Labour, and likewise the Discouragement, Scarcity, and Insufficiency of Tradesmen.[48]

There was complaint in an apprentice law of 1646 that poor parents for the most part were "most averse and unwilling to part with their children," as apprenticeship required, because of their "fond indulgence and perverse obstinacy."[49] This natural parental feeling no doubt persisted, and probably parents who could get along without having to ask for public aid in their support, even though their manner of living was of low grade, objected to having their children taken away from them, especially when the training in apprenticeship was poor and the life of the tradesman unsatisfactory. In consideration of these facts the officials probably generally refrained from using force except in cases where the parents were notorious for their evil living.

The interest in the welfare of neglected children which was expressed by the legislators certainly was not as strong as that in the improvement of industry, and at a time when in England and in Virginia the *laissez faire* doctrine prevailed in matters of public participation in education this interest could not have had much force with the local authorities, particularly when the advantages gained by apprenticeship were not obvious. We have an indication of the lack of interest in the educational welfare of the poor in the lax way in which the endowed schools were managed, and there is a similar indication in the fact that an expenditure of public funds for education in schools was practically never made.

Attention has been confined heretofore to a determination of the relative number of children bound out in forced apprenticeship. Consideration should also be given to various provisions in the indentures and to the extent to which they were carried out, although the fact that relatively few children were bound out lessens the importance of the matter. As in England, the form of contract used was like that in industrial apprenticeship, the master agreeing to teach or cause the apprentice to be taught the "art, trade, or mystery" he was following. During the eighteenth century it was customary, even before the passage of laws requiring it, to stipulate in the agreement that instruction in reading and writing or "schooling" should also be given, although such provision was not made as often in the cases of girls as of boys. How faithfully the masters carried out their agreements cannot be determined at all exactly. The

---

[48]Hartwell, Chilton, and Blair, *The Present State of Virginia* (1697), p. 8.
[49]Hening, I, 336.

supervision of the system of apprenticeship was in the hands of the county justices, and the court records show that they sometimes admonished and punished masters for failure to treat their apprentices as the indentures required.[50] We may assume that the fear of the court or interest in the welfare of their apprentices held a considerable share of the masters to their contracts. It seems likely, however, that if the provisions for schooling and trade education had been customarily held to, a larger number of children would have been bound out.

Several factors which in spite of the provisions in the indentures probably tended to lower the quality and the amount of education received by poor children in apprenticeship may be mentioned. In England the custom was to disregard the educational features in the indentures, and this practice must have had some effect in Virginia. The fact that the provision of support was the primary motive in binding out children suggests that if a master cared for the physical needs of his apprentice and did not abuse him, little in the way of education might be required of him. The custom of binding out children when they were very young, some years before their masters could be expected to pay any attention to their instruction, no doubt tended to obscure the educational object. The relatives or friends of the children were not of the type to exercise much influence favorable to them, and the apprentices probably were not greatly interested in the fulfillment of the educational part of the contracts. While the number of schools in Virginia increased as time went on, the distance of many of the homes from a school must have made it difficult very often for the masters to provide instruction in reading and writing. There was no flourishing system of industrial apprenticeship to set standards of trade education, and there was a tendency on the part of the masters to set their apprentices to raising tobacco to the neglect of their trade instruction.

The trades to which poor boys were most commonly apprenticed, as shown by orders and indentures, were those of carpenter, shoemaker, planter, and blacksmith; but other trades to which they were occasionally bound were those of weaver, tailor, cooper, tanner, bricklayer, joiner, and wheelwright. The indentures of girls commonly required that they should be taught spinning sewing, and knitting, or "household business."

It does not seem to have been the practice for the master to pay

[50]Bruce, *Institutional History of Virginia*, I, pp. 311–14.

freedom dues or to make gifts to the poor apprentice upon the completion of his term of service except in the way of an outfit of clothing and a small amount of food which law and custom required even though the indenture did not so stipulate. A law of 1705 required that at the expiration of the poor orphan apprentice's period of servitude the master should "pay and allow him in like manner as is appointed for servants by indenture or custom,"[51] and in 1727 this provision was made applicable to other poor children.[52] The servants were commonly given a barrel of corn and an equipment of clothing. Most of the indentures found in the parish records make no requirement of freedom dues, and where there was nothing concerning the matter it may be assumed that only the customary food and clothing were given. Occasionally, however, the master was required by the indenture to give more. In 1707 in St. Paul's Parish a master agreed to pay a girl apprentice "Six Hunderd pounds of good sound sweet Tobacco in Cash, when she shall become of age." In 1733 another master agreed to give to two apprentices, a boy and a girl, "unto each of them Five pounds current money and each of them one cow and calf."[53]

SUMMARY

The primary purpose of poor law apprenticeship in colonial Virginia, as in England, was the relief of the public from the costs of maintaining dependent children. A secondary purpose was the upbringing and education of those who were bound out, but in practice the scheme was not looked upon as a device for educating the poor generally and it did not reach any large share of the lower class of people. For the limited number who were bound out under the law it was, considering the conditions, a more or less effective means of trade and literary education.

---

[51]Hening, III, 375.
[52]Hening, IV, 212.
[53]MS. Vestry Minutes, pp. 16, 58.

CHAPTER VI

CONCLUSION

The foregoing study of public education as conducted by the parishes in colonial Virginia has brought out the fact that efforts were confined to an attempt to provide for the instruction and training of the poor. The chief element in the plan outlined in the law was a system of compulsory apprenticeship giving trade training and schooling to dependent children and to those whose parents were negligent or unable because of poverty to give them an education. In addition to apprenticeship as a means of trade education, provision was made for the establishment of county-parish work schools. Custom gave the vestries the right to defray the costs of tuition of poor children in private schools in individual cases where it seemed desirable, and late in the colonial period the vestries were allowed by statute to establish workhouses and to levy a tax for the support of education in them. While endowed schools were not comprehended in the scheme of parish education as outlined in the law, the men who founded such institutions looked upon them as a part of the provision for the poor and commonly gave their administration partially or wholly to parish officials. The work of administering the means of educating the poor was divided throughout most of the colonial period between the county and the parish, but as time went on the parish came to have the larger share of the responsibility.

The scheme of education embracing the means of caring for the education of the poor which have been mentioned was in theory adequate to secure its object. In practice, however, apprenticeship was the only device at all generally used, and most of the children bound out in forced apprenticeship were dependents. The endowed parish-county schools which were next in importance to apprenticeship were not numerous enough to reach any considerable share of the poor children, and they were not managed in such a way as to realize their full possibilities. The other means of parish education provided for in law or recognized in custom were so rarely used as to be negligible. Since the results of our examination of the sources bearing on parish education are so largely negative, it might be thought that perhaps the county, which shared legal responsibility with the parish, was the institution which in practice actually did the work. This possibility has been taken into consideration, however, and it has been shown that it was only in apprenticeship that the county ever acted independently, and that whether the binding out was done by the county or parish officials or by both in co-operation our conclusion that ordinarily only dependents were apprenticed holds. Except for the occasional payment of apprenticeship premiums there was practically no expenditure of public funds for educational purposes in colonial Virginia.

While attention may be called to certain facts to show why there was only a small amount of public activity in education in colonial Virginia there is not the call for an explanation that there would be if the public had participated to a considerable extent. That is, there was no factor in the situation which would lead to the presumption that more was done than a general conformity to English precedents demanded, and that there were reasons for doing less than was done in England can readily be seen. The chief interfering factors were the wide distribution of the population and the frontier conditions which made it difficult to carry out any sort of community enterprise. There was not the strong religious demand for the teaching of reading which was an essential factor in the development of public schools in New England, and the uniformity of belief in the principles of the Established Church meant that there was not the same interest as there was in England in providing orthodox instruction so as to combat the influence of competing sects. The economic interest which was expressed in the legislation dealing with workhouses and apprenticeship was not strong enough to overcome the difficulties inherent in the industrial system. Philanthropic concern in the educational welfare of the poor expressed itself in the form of gifts for the establishment of a number of free schools and endowments for the payment of tuition for instruction in private schools rather than in an effort to secure general public provision for them. Whether the undemocratic character of local government was a factor interfering with the development of education for the poor may be doubted, for there is no evidence of a demand coming from the people who would have been benefitted by it.

When in 1779 Thomas Jefferson undertook his project of establishing a scheme of public education in Virginia there was no precedent upon which he could depend except the custom of parish and county participation in the administration of poor law apprenticeship and endowed schools for the poor. Back of the practice there was an idea that the public should be concerned with the education of the poor, but there was no general feeling of real public responsibility and no sense of an obligation to do anything which might involve the levying of taxes. While what was done in colonial Virginia in the way of public interference in the education of the poor may be viewed as a step toward the later development of common schools, it probably was an obstacle rather than a help. The association of the idea of public education with that of provision for the poor alone made it seem natural in the early part of the federal period to confine the efforts made to an improvement of arrangements for the poor. Such an attempt could not have the enthusiastic backing of any class.

BIBLIOGRAPHY

SOURCE MATERIAL

An Account of Several Workhouses. London, 1732.

Bailey, Wm. *A Treatise on the Better Employment and More Comfortable Support of the Poor in Workhouses.* London, 1758.

Beverley, Robert. *The History and Present State of Virginia.* London, 1705.

Boucher, Jonathan. *Letters from Jonathan Boucher to George Washington.*

Burn, Richard. *History of the Poor Laws.* London, 1764.

Burn, Richard. *The Justice of the Peace and Parish Officer*, London, 1772.

Clews, Elsie. *Educational Legislation and Administration of the Colonial Governments.* New York, 1899.

Dalton, Michael. *The Country Justice.* London, 1746.

Fithian, Philip V. "Journal." *American Historical Review*, Vol. V.

Force, Peter. *Historical Tracts.* Washington, 1836–1846.

Fothergill, Gerald. *A List of Emigrant Ministers to America.* London, 1904.

Hartwell, Chilton, and Blair. *Present State of Virginia.* London, 1697.

Hening, W. W. *Statutes of Virginia.*

Jarratt, Devereux. *Autobiography.* 1806.

Jones, Hugh. *The Present State of Virginia.* London, 1725.

Journals of the House of Burgesses.

Perry, W. S. *Historical Collections Relating to the American Colonial Church.* Vol. I.

Poor laws, or *The Laws and Statutes relating to the Settling, Maintenance, and Employment of the Poor.* London, 1727.

Syms-Eaton Free School.

Virginia Historical Collections.

Virginia Magazine of History and Biography. Richmond, 1894–1922.

William and Mary College Quarterly. 1892–1922.

Parish Vestry Books:

Albemarle in Sussex County, 1741–1784, Episcopal Seminary, Alexandria.

Antrim in Halifax, 1752–1817; Alexandria.

Augusta in Augusta, 1747–1780; County Clerk's Office, Staunton.

Blissland in New Kent, 1721–1787; Alexandria.

Bristol in Prince George, 1720–1789; library of Rev. Churchill Gibson, Richmond; reprint edited by C. G. Chamberlayne.

Bruton in James City; original destroyed; extracts in *Church Review and Ecclesiastical Register*, Vol. VIII, 1855–6.

Christ Church in Lancaster, 1739–1786; Alexandria.

Christ Church in Middlesex, 1663–1887; Alexandria.

Cumberland in Lunenburg, 1747–1784; Alexandria.

93

Dettingen in Prince William, 1748–1802; Alexandria.

Elizabeth City in Elizabeth City, 1751–1780; Rev. C. B. Bryan, Petersburg.

Frederick in Frederick, 1764–1816; Alexandria.

Fredericksville in Louisa, 1742–1787; Alexandria.

Henrico in Henrico, 1730–1773; in possession of vestry of St. John's Church, Richmond; reprint in Wynne's *Historical Documents from the Old Dominion*.

King William in Powhatan (later Henrico), 1707–1750; Miss Lelia Walker, Ft. Estell, Kentucky; translation from French in which record was kept in *Virginia Magazine of History*, Volumes XI, XII, XIII.

Kingston in Mathews, 1679–1796; Alexandria.

Lexington in Amherst, 1779–1880; Alexandria.

Linhaven in Norfolk, 1723–1779; MS. copy, Rev. C. B. Bryan, Petersburg.

Petsworth in Gloucester, 1677–1793; MS. copy, Virginia Historical Society, Richmond.

St. George's in Spottsylvania, 1726–1800; Episcopal rectory, Fredericksburg.

St. James in Goochland, 1744–1860; Alexandria.

St. Mark's in Culpeper, 1730–1778; Alexandria.

St. Paul's in Hanover and New Kent, 1755–1774; Alexandria.

St. Peter's in New Kent, 1686–1759; Alexandria.

Shelburne in Loudon, 1771–1805; Alexandria.

Stratton Major in King and Queen, 1729–1775; Alexandria.

Truro in Fairfax, 1732–1782; Mt. Vernon.

Upper Parish in Nansemond, 1744–1793; Alexandria.

Wicomico in Northumberland, 1703–1795; Alexandria.

GENERAL HISTORIES

Anderson, J. S. M. *History of the Church of England in the Colonies.* Vol. 3. London, 1845.

Ballagh, J. C. *White Servitude in the Colony of Virginia.* J. H. U. Studies, Vol. 13.

Brickell, J. *Natural History of North Carolina.* Dublin, 1737.

Brock. *The Colonial Virginian.* Richmond, 1891.

Bruce, P. A. *Economic History of Virginia in the 17th Century.* 2 vol. New York, 1907.

Bruce, P. A. *Institutional History of Virginia in the 17th Century.* 2 vol. New York, 1910.

Burk, John. *History of Virginia.* 4 vol. 1804.

Channing, Edward. *Town and County Government in Virginia.* J. H. U. Studies, Vol. II.

Colonial Churches of Virginia. Richmond, 1908.

Conway, Moncure D. *Barons of the Potomac and Rappahannock.* New York, 1892.

Dalcho, F. *History of the Episcopal Church in South Carolina.* Charleston, 1820.

Digest of S. P. G. Records, 1701-1892. London, 1893.

Eggleston, Edward. *The Transit of Civilization.* New York, 1901.

Fiske, John. *Old Virginia and Her Neighbors.* 2 vol. Boston, 1897.

Gray, B. K. *A History of English Philanthropy.* London, 1905.

Ingle, Edward. *Local Institutions of Virginia.* J. H. U. Studies, 1885.

Leonard, E. M. *The Early History of English Poor Relief.* Cambridge, 1900.
Meade, W. G. *Old Churches and Families of Virginia.* Philadelphia, 1861.
Nicholls, Geo. *History of the English Poor Law.* New York, 1898. 2 v.
Osgood, H. L. *The American Colonies in the 17th Century.* 3 vol. New York, 1904.
Schuricht. *History of the German Element in Virginia.* Baltimore, 1898.
Stanard, Mary M. P. *Colonial Virginia.* Philadelphia, 1917.
Webb, Sidney. *English Local Government.* London, 1906.
Wertenbaker, T. J. *Virginia under the Staurts.* Princeton, 1914.
Wilberforce, Samuel. *History of the Protestant Episcopal Church in America.* New York, 1849.

HISTORIES OF EDUCATION

Cubberley, E. P. *Public Education in the United States.* Boston, 1919.
Dunlop, O. J. *English Apprenticeship.* London, 1912.
Graves, F. P. *History of Education in Modern Times.* New York, 1915.
Jackson, G. L. *School Support in Colonial Massachusetts.* New York, 1909.
Kemp, W. W. *Support of Schools in Colonial New York by the S. P. G.* New York, 1913.
Leach, E. *Early Yorkshire Schools.* Leeds, 1899.
McCabe, W. G. *Virginia Schools before the Revolution.* 1890.
Maddox, W. A. *The Free School Idea in Virginia.* New York, 1918.
de Montmorency, J. E. G. *State Interference in English Education.* Cambridge, 1902.
Monroe, Paul (Editor). *Cyclopedia of Education.*
Steiner, B. C. *History of Education in Maryland.* Washington, 1894.
Watson, Foster. *English Grammar Schools to 1680.* Cambridge, 1908.

LOCAL HISTORIES

Goodwin, W. A. R. *Historical Sketch of Bruton Church.* Williamsburg, 1903.
Lysons, D. *Environs of London.* 4. vol. London, 1792.
Slaughter, Philip. *History of St. Mark's Parish.* Baltimore, 1877.
Slaughter, Philip. *History of Truro Parish.* Philadelphia, 1908.
Scott, W. W. *A History of Orange County, Virginia.* Richmond, 1907.
Tyler, L. C. *Williamsburg, the Old Colonial Capital.* Richmond, 1907.
Waddell, J. A. *Annals of Augusta County.* Richmond, 1886.
Wayland, J. W. *A History of Rockingham County, Virginia.* Dayton, Va., 1912.
Wise, J. C. *Early History of the Eastern Shore.* Richmond, 1911.

BIOGRAPHY

Beveridge, A. J. *The Life of John Marshall.* Vol. I. New York, 1916.
Brown, Alexander. *The Cabells and Their Kin.* Boston, 1895.
Pryor, Mrs. Roger A. *The Mother of Washington and Her Times.* New York, 1903.
Rives, W. C. *Life and Times of James Madison.* Boston, 1859.

VITA

GUY F. WELLS was born in Oakfield, Wisconsin, January 5, 1880.

Academic Training: Oakfield High School, 1894–1898; State Normal School, Oshkosh, Wisconsin, 1898–1900; Chicago University, 1900–01; Columbia University, 1906–10, 1920–21;

Professional Experience: High School teacher, two years; teacher in Ethical Culture School, New York, 1903–06; University of Wisconsin, instructor, 1910–13; Rhode Island Normal School, instructor, 1913–20; New York Training School, instructor, 1921–23; lecturer in summer session, University of Chicago (1915), University of Wisconsin (1921), Peabody College (1922).